THE LAW

of the

YIELD

THE LAW
of the
YIELD

The Highest Law of Successful Living

Greg McClanahan

TATE PUBLISHING
AND **ENTERPRISES**, LLC

Published by Tate Publishing & Enterprises, LLC
127 E. Trade Center Terrace | Mustang, Oklahoma 73064 USA
1.888.361.9473 | www.tatepublishing.com

Tate Publishing is committed to excellence in the publishing industry. The company reflects the philosophy established by the founders, based on Psalm 68:11,
"The Lord gave the word and great was the company of those who published it."

Book design copyright © 2013 by Tate Publishing, LLC. All rights reserved.
Cover design by Jan Sunday Quilaquil
Interior design by Honeylette Pino

Published in the United States of America

ISBN: 978-1-62510-129-7
1. Self-Help / General
2. Self-Help / Personal Growth / Success
13.08.02

DEDICATION

To my wonderful parents, Butch and Jean
McClanahan. Thank you for planting
the seeds of success in my life.

———◆———

To my amazing wife, Toni. Thank you for
inspiring me to strive to be my best. I hope that
someday I can catch up and be more like you.

———◆———

To my remarkable children. Thank you
for being the highlight of my life.

ACKNOWLEDGMENTS

There are many people that I need to thank for helping me write this book. I hope you will bear with me as my heart pauses for a few moments to acknowledge the people that have inspired me and supported me throughout the writing of this work.

I find inspiration in the stories and examples of others that show greatness in their daily life by just doing the right thing. I am moved by great authors, cinematographers, lyricists, athletes on the field of play, and by each of you that I see down the path of life I travel each day. There are so many unnameable individuals that lift me to higher ground. To you, I owe a debt of gratitude for teaching me how to live a better life.

I am greatly influenced by those closest to me that have shaped my life—my mom and dad, my siblings, my wife and children, friends and business associates. I am grateful that my family supported me as I spent many months working on this book and all they saw of me was the back of my head while I sat at my computer deep into the night. To you, I owe my deepest happiness.

During the many hours of writing and editing, I have read and reread every sentence. I often look at the words in wonder. I could not have expressed these ideas in such a way without the inspiration of God. I believe the content and ideas are inspired by him and can therefore be of benefit to every reader. To God, I owe everything.

Lastly, I want to thank Tate Publishing for accepting my manuscript and believing in its potential to make a difference.

CONTENTS

Preface 13

Introduction... 17

Chapter I: The Law of the Harvest...................... 21

Chapter II: The Law of the Yield........................ 37

Chapter III: Building a Life with Yield in Mind ... 59

Chapter IV: Rearview Mirror 75

Chapter V: The Quick Response Award 81

Chapter VI: Yield in Action................................. 87

Chapter VII: Moving Forward 195

Nothing could be worse than the fear that one had given up too soon, and left one unexpended effort that might have saved the world.

—Jane Addams

It's not that some people have willpower and some don't. It's that some people are ready to change, and others are not.

—Heraclitus

PREFACE

I am drawn to write this book out of a desire to share what I have discovered about successful living. I am often inspired by a story, a book, a movie, or the music and lyrics in a song. When I feel that inspiration, I am grateful for the talents of others who help me move my life to higher ground.

I believe it is possible for each of us to make a positive difference in someone else's life. I believe it is not only possible, but I believe it is our duty to try.

I have been influenced by the things I've learned from others as well as my own experiences. My work experience has taken me through being the son of a grocery store owner, a pizza delivery driver, an airline reservation agent, a corporate trainer, a sales professional, a business owner, and a personal and organizational development consultant. Throughout these decades, I slowly discovered the missing link in helping myself, my employees, and my clients perform at the highest levels of excellence and motivation. My most important role as a father and now a grandfather makes me look longingly at a way to perpetuate this knowledge to my posterity and to all who truly want the most from their life.

It is interesting to me that there are only twenty-six letters in the alphabet which create the thousands of words that fill a standard dictionary. The challenge for any writer is to find the right words and to arrange them in just the right order to communicate their message and to inspire the reader. It is my sincerest desire that this work will be enjoyable for you to read but more importantly that it will offer insights that will help you in every area of your life as you pursue your personal and professional best.

I do not believe there is another personal or organizational development book that combines the resources of so many inspiring stories and practical examples of people caught in the act of living their best. This format provides a roadmap that you can choose to follow in creating a life of excellence—a life that will *yield* limitless bushels of goodness and success.

Your life does not get better by chance, it gets better by change.

—Jim Rohn

The most important thing is to be able at any moment to sacrifice who you are for what you can become.

—Charles Dubois

The greater danger for most of us is not that our aim is too high and we miss it, but it is too low, and we reach it.

—Michelangelo Buonarroti

INTRODUCTION

This book introduces the law of the yield and further describes how to use it to your advantage in achieving the highest levels of personal, professional, and organizational excellence.

There are specific laws that govern our lives. For example, the law of the harvest is that "whatsoever you sow, that is what you will also reap." If you want to harvest wheat, you must plant seeds of wheat. The earth will only produce a harvest that corresponds to the seeds that are sown.

Similar are the seeds within our character. If you plant kindness, you will harvest friendships; and if you plant truth, learning, and experience, you will harvest wisdom.

The law of gravity teaches us that if you drop a rock from a building, it will always go down, never up. The law of maintaining your health requires exercise and good nutrition. The law of supply and demand leads to an understanding of financial markets.

It is when you understand these laws that you can work within their boundaries and apply them to your advantage and success.

As we understand more about the law of the harvest, the question that arises is "Why is the *yield* so varied by each individual at harvest time?" The laws of nature continue to prove that what we do prior to planting, during the actual process of planting and the nurturing process after planting will influence the *yield*. Identical seed, soil, crop, and weather conditions might yield thirty bushels of wheat per acre for one farmer while another may realize a one hundred bushel per acre yield. Why? The secret lies in the law of the yield.

More important than simply learning the laws of success, you must learn how to apply them to daily events. So if you desire the maximum *yield* in your life, you will find the secret within these pages. You will understand and know how to apply the law of the yield to every area of your life, career, and organization. The law of the yield reveals the instructions of how to apply the law of the harvest at the highest level.

In *The Contented Achiever*, Don Hutson, George Lucas, and Chris Crouch state, "You must have a profound understanding of the principles that influence your life. And if you are serious about creating the life that you desire, you must become a master at applying your knowledge to daily events. By [so] doing, you can get from where you are to where you want to be."

The intent of this book is to not only help you gain an appreciation of the principles associated with the law of the yield but to also provide practical examples of these principles in action. Thereby, you will be able to obtain an intellectual understanding of the law, but more importantly, you will see these principles in action and can understand how to apply them to the daily events in your own life.

The law of the yield touches every area of your life. You will discover that this law deserves your utmost attention. Don't allow yourself to become so busy doing good things that you miss out on your best.

One ship drives east and another drives west
With the selfsame winds that blow,
Tis the set of the sails,
And not the gales,
That tell us the way to go.
Like the winds of the sea, are the ways of fate;
As you voyage along through life,
Tis the set of a soul
That determines its goal,
And not the calm or the strife.

—Ella Wheeler Wilcox

THE LAW
OF THE HARVEST

I was raised in a small farming community in Southwest Colorado. In this setting, the law of the harvest was an everyday reality. From this agricultural setting, it was simple to understand this law in that whatsoever you sow, that is what you will also reap. If a farmer desired to harvest wheat, then wheat seed was planted.

As I grew older, I began to realize how this law applies to every area of life and business. If you desire to harvest respect, you must sow within your character the seeds of integrity and honesty. If you want to harvest accomplishment, you must sow accountability. You must sow gratitude if you want to harvest higher levels of cooperation and increased effort within your organization.

The foundation of your success will come from gaining an understanding and awareness of the harvest that comes from each seed you sow in your life and character. If you are harvest driven, determine what or who you want to become and then work backward to find the corresponding seeds that must be planted in order to realize your desired harvest.

Regardless of what you plant, the corresponding harvest will always grow in kind and is always predictable. If you plant seeds of trust, you will harvest relationships; but conversely, if you plant discord, you will never harvest cooperation. You cannot control the harvest; you can only control the seeds you sow. The harvest takes care of itself.

There is beauty in this law because it does not discriminate. If you are rich or poor, young or old, tall or short, the law is constant. It is up to you to create the life you want and to take charge of your future.

What are some of the things you might want to harvest in your life? Stronger friendships, a promotion at work, financial independence, increased love in your marriage, or maybe a better self-image?

Ralph Waldo Emerson understood the seed to harvest relationships when he said,

> sow a thought and you reap an action;
> Sow an act and you reap a habit;
> Sow a habit and you reap a character;
> Sow a character and you reap a destiny.

For the law of the harvest to be useful in your life, you must seek out and understand the seed-to-harvest relationships that govern the universe. Over the decades, wonderful schools of thought concerning the keys to success have been introduced. Dr. Norman Vincent Peale promoted the power of positive thinking and Earl Nightingale expounded upon the idea that "we become what we think about." Others promote the idea that to accomplish positive outcomes, you must speak positive words about your future. Stephen Covey in *The 7 Habits of Highly Effective People* describes that transformation occurs from the "inside-out."

There are important and valuable lessons we can glean from these and many other ideas, but the questions that often remain unanswered are the following: What should I think about? What are the words I should speak? What are the things that I need to work on to achieve the character traits I desire to possess on the inside?

To answer these questions, you must discover the seeds that must be planted in order to realize your desired harvest. Positive thinking is one of the many seeds as is the need to speak positive words, but they are only two of many seeds that must be considered when planting.

To give you some idea of what this means on a practical level, the following are some possible seed-to-harvest relationships:

- To harvest potential, you must plant belief.
- To harvest understanding, you must plant communication.
- To harvest success, you must plant value.
- To harvest cooperation, you must plant gratitude.
- To harvest appreciation, you must plant recognition.
- To harvest leadership, you must plant love.
- To harvest perfection, you must plant fundamentals and practice.
- To harvest excitement, you must plant enthusiasm.
- To harvest growth, you must plant change.
- To harvest love, you must plant compassion.
- To harvest compassion, you must plant service.

- To harvest relationships, you must plant selflessness.
- To harvest accomplishment, you must plant task management.
- To harvest professionalism, you must plant expertise.
- To harvest a lasting relationship with your children, you must plant discipline, but you must also plant friendship.
- To harvest innovation, you must plant creativity.
- To harvest creativity, you must plant imagination.
- To harvest fulfillment, you must plant hope.
- To harvest knowledge, you must plant learning.
- To harvest change, you must plant action.
- To harvest stability, you must plant balance.
- To harvest a legacy, you must plant responsibility.
- To harvest a positive culture, you must plant optimism.
- To harvest goodness, you must plant goodness.
- To harvest accomplishment, you must plant goals.
- To harvest productivity, you must plant potential.
- To harvest a following, you must plant leadership.
- To harvest inspiration, you must plant vision.
- To harvest greatness, you must plant hard work.
- To harvest healing, you must plant forgiveness.
- To harvest prosperity, you must plant discipline.
- To harvest honor, you must plant courage.
- To harvest persistence, you must plant resiliency.
- To harvest wisdom, you must plant applied knowledge.

- To harvest affection, you must plant sensitivity.
- To harvest self-respect, you must plant values.
- To harvest good health, you must plant good nutrition and exercise.
- To harvest loyalty, you must plant encouragement and honesty.
- To harvest value, you must plant sharing.
- To harvest success, you must plant growth.
- To harvest integrity, you must plant virtue.
- To harvest understanding, you must plant empathy.
- To harvest courage, you must plant confidence.
- To harvest purity, you must plant self-control.
- To harvest accomplishment, you must plant dreams and desire.
- To harvest more clients, you must plant expertise and responsiveness.
- To harvest confidence, you must plant trust.
- To harvest action, you must plant motivation.
- To harvest adoration, you must plant sincerity.
- To harvest kindness, you must plant gentleness.
- To harvest respect, you must plant integrity.
- To harvest self-confidence, you must plant humility.
- To harvest patience, you must plant perseverance.
- To harvest affection, you must plant relationships.
- To harvest fulfillment, you must plant charity.
- To harvest action, you must plant responsiveness.
- To harvest friendships, you must plant kindness and understanding.

- To harvest a brighter future, you must plant hope.
- To harvest unity, you must plant compromise.
- To harvest productivity, you must plant encouragement.
- To harvest success, you must plant courage.
- To harvest character, you must plant sacrifice.
- To harvest joy, confidence, and strength, you must plant faith.
- To harvest miracles, you must plant hope.
- To harvest wisdom, you must plant truth.
- To harvest nobility, you must plant wisdom.
- To harvest meekness, you must plant humility.
- To harvest inspiration, you must plant prayer.
- To harvest happiness, you must plant meaning.
- To harvest laughter, you must plant peace.

Conversely, you must realize that just as the law of the harvest works to your benefit, it will also work to your downfall. Therefore you must realize that

- if you sow pride, you will harvest contention;
- if you sow selfishness, you will harvest loneliness;
- if you sow abuse, you will harvest addiction;
- if you sow anger, you will harvest resentment;
- if you sow arrogance, you will harvest separation; and
- if you sow nothing, you will harvest hopelessness.

There are many more seeds to be planted within your character that will allow you to realize a specific harvest. If you desire a particular harvest, you must discover, plant, and nurture the corresponding seeds. Become a student of your desired harvest, and it will become clear as to what corresponding seeds you must plant in order to realize that harvest. It is clear that your harvest is predicated upon the seeds you plant. That is the formula, that is the law, and the law never fails.

Sadly, you can complete an entire college curriculum in preparation for your career and not be taught how to foster meaningful relationships that will truly mark your ability to be successful within the workplace. You might create a well-defined company value statement and yet not know how to make it transform your organization. Until you understand the significance of planting the appropriate seeds that will produce your desired harvest, there will be voids in your ability to live the life you desire and achieve the highest levels of success.

It is said that "money will buy a fine dog, but only kindness will make him wag his tail."

Planted Seed = Corresponding Harvest

Within your life or organization, it is important to realize that there is a planting season and a time in the future when you will reap a harvest. Some seeds grow quickly while others take time to grow. For example, the seeds of gratitude can positively affect cooperation immediately while the fruit of respect may take a full growing season to realize.

You must understand that you cannot reap where you have not sown. A harvest will not come if you have not planted. If you think respect will come to you from being given the title of "manager," the laws of nature teach otherwise. You cannot harvest a deep and abiding respect from your colleagues if you have not yet sown the seeds required to achieve this harvest.

It is important to also note that you must be aware of what seeds are being planted by others in your life or organization. If you see the seeds of gossip floating through the air, they can easily take root like a bad weed and envy and discord will compromise the harvest of the positive seeds you've planted. Although it can be difficult at times, you must pull the weeds in order to allow the good seeds in your life to flourish.

Just as a wheat farmer must plant seeds each year, you must also continually sow the same seeds of greatness if you want to continue to reap your desired harvest. Just because you have realized the harvest of affection in your marriage does not mean that you can stop planting the seeds of fidelity, sensitivity, and tolerance. You must consistently plant and replant those seeds in order to continue reaping the associated harvest.

Aristotle said, "We are what we repeatedly do. Excellence, therefore, is not an act but a habit." And Henry L. Doherty said, "Plenty of men can do good work for a spurt and with immediate promotion in mind, but for promotion, you want a man in whom good work has become a habit." Don't delay in this process; the seed of procrastination will produce no harvest.

Remember, you get to choose what you will plant, but you do not get to choose the harvest; it takes care of itself. The law of the harvest teaches us that there is significance in every choice! Every seed we choose to plant, every thought and every action carries with it an associated harvest. Its power must be harnessed to your benefit or its power will work toward your demise. The law does not discriminate and therefore can work to everyone's benefit in equal proportion.

I believe the following story provides an important lesson and one that further defines the principles explained through the law of the harvest.

CARL'S GARDEN

Carl was a quiet man. He would always greet you with a big smile and a firm handshake. Even after living in our neighborhood for over fifty years, no one could really say they knew him very well.

Before his retirement, he took the bus to work each morning. The lone sight of him walking down the street often worried us. He had a slight limp from a bullet wound received in WWII. Watching him, we worried that although he had survived WWII, he may not make it through our changing uptown neighborhood with its ever-increasing random violence, gangs, and drug activity.

When he saw the flyer at our local church asking for volunteers for caring for the gardens behind the minister's residence, he responded in his characteristically unassuming manner. Without fanfare, he just signed up.

He was well into his eighty-seventh year when the very thing we had always feared finally happened. He was just finishing his watering for the day when three gang members approached him. Ignoring their attempt to intimidate him, he simply asked, "Would you like a drink from the hose?"

The tallest and toughest looking of the three said, "Yeah, sure," with a malevolent little smile. As Carl offered the hose to him, the other two grabbed Carl's arm, throwing him down. As the hose snaked crazily over the ground, dousing everything in its way, Carl's assailants stole his retirement watch and wallet, and then fled.

Carl tried to get himself up, but he had been thrown down on his bad leg. He lay there, trying to gather himself as the minister came running to help him. Although the minister had witnessed the attack from his window, he couldn't get there fast enough to stop it.

"Carl, are you okay? Are you hurt?" the minister kept asking as he helped Carl to his feet.

Carl just passed a hand over his brow and sighed, shaking his head. "Just some kids. I hope they'll wise up someday."

His wet clothes clung to his slight frame as he bent to pick up the hose. He adjusted the nozzle again and started to water. Confused and a little concerned, the minister asked, "Carl, what are you doing?"

"I've got to finish my watering. It's been very dry lately," came the calm reply. Satisfying himself that Carl really was all right, the minister could only marvel. Carl was a man from a different time and place.

A few weeks later, the three returned. Just as before, their threat was unchallenged. Carl again offered them a drink from his hose. This time, they didn't rob him. They wrenched the hose from his hand and drenched him head to foot in the icy water.

When they had finished their humiliation of him, they sauntered off down the street, throwing catcalls and curses, falling over one another laughing at the hilarity of what they had just done. Carl just watched them. Then he turned toward the warmth giving sun, picked up his hose, and went on with his watering.

The summer was quickly fading into fall. Carl was doing some tilling when he was startled by the sudden approach of someone behind him. He stumbled and fell into some evergreen branches. As he struggled to regain his footing, he turned to see the tall leader of his summer tormentors reaching down for him. He braced himself for the expected attack.

"Don't worry. I'm not gonna hurt you this time." The young man spoke softly, still offering the tattooed and scarred hand to Carl. As he helped Carl get up, the man pulled a crumpled bag from his pocket and handed it to Carl.

"What's this?" Carl asked.

"It's your stuff," the man explained. "It's your stuff back. Even the money in your wallet."

"I don't understand," Carl said. "Why would you help me now?"

The man shifted his feet, seeming embarrassed and ill at ease. "I learned something from you," he said. "I ran with that gang and hurt people like you. We picked you because you were old and we knew we could do it. But every time we came and did something to you, instead of yelling and fighting back, you tried to give us a drink. You didn't hate us for hating you. You kept showing love against our hate."

He stopped for a moment. "I couldn't sleep after we stole your stuff, so here it is back."

He paused for another awkward moment, not knowing what more there was to say. "That bag's my way of saying thanks for straightening me out, I guess." And with that, he walked off down the street.

Carl looked down at the sack in his hands and gingerly opened it. He took out his retirement watch and put it back on his wrist. Opening his wallet, he checked for his wedding photo. He gazed for a moment at the young bride that still smiled back at him from all those years ago.

He died one cold day after Christmas that winter. Many people attended his funeral in spite of the weather. In particular, the minister noticed a tall young man that he didn't know sitting quietly in a distant corner of the church.

The minister spoke of Carl's garden as a lesson in life. In a voice made thick with unshed tears, he said, "Do your best and make your garden as beautiful as you can. We will never forget Carl and his garden."

The following spring another flyer went up. It read, "Person needed to care for Carl's garden."

The flyer went unnoticed by the busy parishioners until one day when a knock was heard at the minister's office door.

Opening the door, the minister saw a pair of scarred and tattooed hands holding the flyer. "I believe this is my job, if you'll have me," the young man said. The minister recognized him as the same young man who had returned the stolen watch and wallet to Carl.

He knew that Carl's kindness had turned this man's life around. As the minister handed him the keys to the garden shed, he said, "Yes, go take care of Carl's garden and honor him."

The man went to work and, over the next several years, he tended the flowers and vegetables just as Carl had done. During that time, he went to college, got married, and became a prominent member of the community. But he never forgot his promise to Carl's memory and kept the garden as beautiful as he thought Carl would have kept it.

One day, he approached the minister and told him that he couldn't care for the garden any longer. He explained with a shy and happy smile, "My wife just had a baby boy last night, and she's bringing him home on Saturday."

"Well, congratulations!" said the minister as he was handed the garden shed keys. "That's wonderful! What's the baby's name?"

"Carl," he replied.

—Unknown Author Found on multiple websites including www.inspire21.com

❧

The way Carl lived his life was as beautiful as the flowers in his garden. He continually planted the seeds of respect, kindness, and pure intentions and exemplified them by the way he treated everyone. How marvelous to see that we have the power within us, at any age, to make a difference in others lives when they simply observe the way we "tend to our garden."

The law of the harvest is reinforced by Carl's story. We learn that if you sow kindness or discord, generosity or selfishness, gratitude or impatience, that is what you will harvest.

Therefore, you must carefully select the seeds you sow in the garden of your life called your character. You never know who will bear your name because the hope of a parent is that their child will grow up to be just like you.

It is impossible to survive the storms and calamities of life without courage. It is the coat of character that we wear into the storm.

—Rick Ezell

He which soweth sparingly shall reap also sparingly; and he which soweth bountifully shall reap also bountifully.

2 Corinthians 9:6
The Apostle Paul

THE LAW
OF THE YIELD

I often wondered what made the difference between someone who is accredited with many accomplishments to someone who realizes moderate success to someone who lives in mediocrity. What causes one business in a community to thrive while an equal and capable competitor closes its doors? In other words, why is the *yield* so varied?

I believe that the secret to one's level of success aligns itself in direct proportion to their understanding and application of the law of the harvest and the law of the yield.

As we learned earlier, the law of the harvest states that whatsoever you sow, that is what you will also reap. The law of the yield is that-

**Whatsoever you sow and continually nurture,
will produce a greater harvest.**

The law of the yield works in conjunction with the law of the harvest. The key to an increased harvest or yield comes from knowing what to do in every season. Knowing what to do prior to planting, after planting, and even up until the time when your harvest is safe in its storehouse. There is never a day that passes in which your harvest is not influenced by your effort and choices. In every instant—every moment—you are influencing the quantity and quality of your *yield* at harvest time.

The tendency of human nature is to be satisfied with a harvest of any proportion. The law of the yield clearly teaches us that we must continue to nurture the seeds we've planned if we expect a bounteous harvest. There are no shortcuts. As referenced in the previous chapter, if you want to harvest cooperation throughout your organization, you must plant appreciation. However, if you want to achieve the highest levels of cooperation—the highest *yield*—you must also continue to plant and nurture other seeds like respect, compassion, selflessness, recognition, and responsiveness. The more aware you become of the seeds that must be planted and nourished to achieve your desired harvest, the better you will become at producing greater yields.

You cannot expect to successfully create a culture of cooperation throughout your organization by gathering everyone together one day and announcing that "interdepartmental cooperation will now be required!" It may produce external results for a few hours, but to change the very fabric of your culture, you must follow the law. It will require you to first plant the right seeds, and then you must provide continual nourishment for their growth before you will begin to see an increased yield in the level of cooperation. Make sure you've planted the seed of vision so that you can be patient and persistent in achieving your desired outcomes.

As an example, let's say your desired harvest is to increase customer loyalty. A couple of seeds that you often see planted by retailers are a rewards program and periodic sales promotions. However, to achieve a greater customer loyalty yield, you could improve your service levels by planting seeds of responsiveness and seeds of follow-up. To establish yourself as an expert and the leader in your industry, the seed of a bi-monthly or monthly newsletter may set you apart from your competitors. Staff training is a key seed to plant that would produce more qualified employees and thus more consumer confidence would result. To retain trained and qualified employees, you'll need to plant the seeds of recognition, gratitude, rewards and appreciation. You must continually plant and nurture these many seeds to produce a culture of cooperation and excellence all of which will yield greater and greater levels of customer loyalty.

There is a formula to improve your yield. It is to properly plant and continually nurture the right seeds within your life and organization. The highest yield of customer loyalty, for example, is available to any organization that has planted all the right seeds. Excellence is a matter of properly managing the planting to harvest process.

This idea is reinforced by the North Dakota State University Extension Service. The years of 1985 and 1992 presented ideal weather conditions for achieving the highest wheat yields in recent history. The reason these years were ideal was because there was cooler growing season weather.

The Extension Office states, "The maximum wheat yield for a given year is going to depend on environment and management to coincide with the opportunities the environment brings. Wheat is a cool season plant and will yield better when the seasons are cool. When the season is favorable for wheat, good management needs to accompany favorable weather." In these peak years, those who were good managers realized a harvest of as much as two hundred bushels per acre.

We must again ask, Why is it that in these years of ideal weather conditions, one farmer's yield was 125 bushels of wheat per acre while his neighbor harvested two hundred? Why is it that in the same community and business climate, one business service succeeds while a competitor fails? Why is it that one individual seems to always have things go their way while their neighbor struggles year after year? Again, we must look to the laws of success.

Unlike a farmer who cannot control the weather and its effect on their yield, you can influence and manage the environment in your life and organization. You can influence the climate and culture regardless of the weather outside. This means that it is possible for you to positively influence the yield of every seed you plant and any harvest you desire. Higher yields are within your reach.

There is a requirement within the growing process for you to spend the necessary time preparing your soil for planting. You must understand your soil, the climate in which you live, and the associated growing cycles. You must select the right variety of seeds and make sure you are planting what you truly desire to harvest.

You must realize that if your life's environment resembles Michigan, you will not be able to grow bananas. If that is what you desire to grow, you must create an environment that resembles the tropics. It is necessary for you to take charge of your life and realize that you are able to change your current environment in order to create the life you desire. The secret lies within the seeds you sow.

Don't overcomplicate this process or feel that it is too involved to even know where to begin. It is as simple as determining a single desired harvest and planting the corresponding seeds. Nourish them daily all the while considering other seeds to plant that will continue to help you realize a greater and greater yield in every area of your life.

Anything worth doing requires the seeds of commitment, faith, and persistence. You must realize that the process of increasing your yield in every area of your life can become more complex as you strive to understand the different characteristics of each seed and harvest. Our lives and organizations are dynamic and multidimensional. This requires you to develop the ability to understand and balance the many character traits that make up a life of greatness and the associated seeds that must be regularly planted.

In other words, you are not just planting one crop of wheat but rather you are planting an entire garden. This requires you to understand how to create the environment that is best suited for each seed in your life or organization. You must become familiar with the requirements to grow and produce the highest yield from every type of seed. Building an organization or living a life with yield in mind is possible and within your reach, but you must become a master farmer.

As a child, I can remember the garden we planted every year on the south side of our home. This was the ideal location because the south side of our property was unobstructed from trees and the sun was present all day long.

Lettuce was one of the first crops we could begin to harvest while an ear of corn was one of the last things that could be pulled from its stock. We planted tomatoes in pots inside our home to get them started when spring conditions outside were still too cold for planting. When the time was right, we transplanted them to the outdoors. I learned that each crop had a different growing cycle and that we would not be able to harvest everything at the same time. Corn was my favorite, but more water and nurturing was required to bring about its harvest.

The seeds of life are more diverse than the seeds of nature, but they respond according to a proven law that to understand will transform your life or organization. Some of the greatest personal and organizational harvests may take a considerable amount of nurturing, but that is what makes them taste so sweet as you begin to realize the fruits of your labor. In the meantime, you can enjoy the harvest of smaller crops that grow faster. It is important that you enjoy the accomplishment of increasing your yield through even the smallest of seeds that you have planted.

When my youngest daughter got her learner's permit and I began driving with her, it reminded me of the hours I had spent with all my children in teaching them how to be safe drivers. As a passenger, my daughter did not pay attention to most of the driver responsibilities that are now required of her. She is beginning to realize that she must look beyond the road immediately ahead and pay attention to all road signs, road hazards, traffic lights, and pedestrians. She is also learning the importance of anticipating other driver's actions so that she can make adjustments as needed.

She is figuring out the mechanics of the car— acceleration, braking, using bright and dim lights, cruise control, and a number of other features. The only thing she knew how to completely operate as a passenger was the stereo; however, as the driver, she has to understand a lot more. It's not been easy for her in the beginning, but she is excited about the day when she will be able to come and go as she wants without having to ask for a ride.

I believe there are similarities in our personal life and profession. Some of us remain in the passenger seat of life far too long. Some of us allow other people, public opinion, and the economy to drive us rather than getting behind the wheel and taking charge of our own direction. It is when you begin to understand that you can, and must, control your own destiny and yield that you leave the passenger seat and take responsibility for the course you will travel through life as the driver. Clearly, if you are a passenger, you cannot control your destination or future.

I know very few people who do not desire to give their best every day. To become your best and produce the greatest yield, you cannot choose at any time to be a passenger. You must be the driver everywhere you go. If you are not positively and consistently nurturing and driving your character, you will compromise your ability to give your best. If you are not nurturing and driving a positive culture in your business, you are compromising your collective yield as an organization.

If you feel like there are parts of your life that you are not driving, slide behind the steering wheel, adjust the seat and mirrors, buckle up, and map your course.

Nido Qubein said, "Regardless of where you were born or what your financial position in life, the power to affect your own future lies within your own hands. Your present circumstances don't determine where you can go; they merely determine where you start."

You must realize that increasing your yield rarely occurs through large events. You can make your life and your business better through simple acts of character each day. Milestones are achieved over time and through small steps. Regardless of your present circumstances, start where you are, and take control of the steering wheel toward the life you desire.

I am reminded of a driving story that provides additional insight to this subject. As you drive through life, it is important to make sure you know that having balance is a part of living a life with yield in mind. You must keep your eyes open for opportunities to help others. It is easy to pass by something significant you can do for someone else if you aren't conscientious about those around you.

In the following story, Josh didn't even know he was passing by someone who needed his help until…

THE BRICK

About ten years ago, a young and very successful executive named Josh was traveling down a Chicago neighborhood street. He was going a bit too fast in his sleek black twelve-cylinder Jaguar XKE, which was only two months old.

As he approached a denser portion of this residential neighborhood, he slowed down and was watching for kids that might dart out from between parked cars. He slowed down a bit more when he thought he saw something near one of the cars. As his car passed, no child darted out, but a brick sailed out and—*wham!*— it smashed into his Jag's shiny black side door!

Screech! Brakes slammed! Gears ground into reverse, and tires madly spun the Jaguar back to the spot from where the brick had been thrown.

Josh jumped out of the car, grabbed the kid, and pushed him up against a parked car. He shouted at the kid, "What was that all about, and who are you? Just what the heck are you doing?"

Building up a head of steam, he went on. "That's my new Jag. That brick you threw is gonna cost you a lot of money. Why did you throw it?"

"Please, mister, please… I'm sorry! I didn't know what else to do!" pleaded the youngster. "I threw the brick because no one else would stop!"

Tears were dripping down the boy's chin as he pointed around the parked car.

"It's my brother, mister," he said. "He rolled off the curb and fell out off his wheelchair, and I can't lift him up."

Sobbing, the boy asked the executive, "Would you please help me get him back into his wheelchair? He's hurt and he's too heavy for me."

Moved beyond words, the young executive tried desperately to swallow the rapidly swelling lump in his throat. Straining, he lifted the young man back into his wheelchair and took out his handkerchief and wiped the scrapes and cuts. He checked to see that everything was okay and made sure they would be able to make it the rest of the way home. He then paused a little longer and watched the younger brother push the wheelchair down the sidewalk.

It was a long walk back to the sleek, shining black twelve-cylinder Jaguar XKE—a long and slow walk. Josh never did fix the side door of his Jaguar. He kept the dent to remind him not to go through life so fast that someone has to throw a brick at him to get his attention.

—Unknown Author Found on multiple
websites including www.booksie.com

My advice is to be mindful of the law, don't let detours distract you, stay between the lines and never let someone else drive your life!

In nature, there are proven processes that aid a farmer in obtaining higher crop yields. He must be willing to learn something new from each year's yield in comparison to prior years. He must figure out what he may have done differently in the management and nurturing process that created a greater or lesser yield.

This is true in life. You must become a student of the nurturing process. You must be able to compare your current yield to what is possible. If you are not positively nurturing your character, you are compromising your yield. The same is true in any organization. You must continually and consistently nurture a positive and healthy company culture and weed out the negatives, or it will slip away without you even realizing it happened.

In *Tiger Traits*, Dr. Nate Booth writes, "In business, we must learn again and again what's important in any situation, so we can pay attention to the small things that will have the biggest impact."

For example, personality profile testing can be one of the most beneficial assessments that you can perform as a leader. Not only is it helpful to know each employee's dominant personality type, it is important to know how your personality type will interact with all others. This may lead you to plant one seed for one employee while a different seed is required for another in order to achieve the same results. You must use all the available tools that can help you best assess the seeds that must be sown in order to achieve your desired harvest.

There are things that we know about the way we learn as well as the way we forget. Mastery of a skill or talent comes from continual repetition and practice—nurturing. The longer it has been since you have had exposure to, or use of, a particular skill, the less likely you are to remember it at the very moment when it would have made all the difference. Continual nurturing of your character is the key to living a life that will produce the highest yield.

An example of this is demonstrated by my oldest daughter. She learned to play the piano with some proficiency in her younger years. She became busy with other activities after entering high school and piano took a back seat. It has now been a number of years since she has played and those familiar songs and skills are forgotten.

If you have ever attended a seminar or training event, you will likely recall the excitement it may have generated among the attendees, but soon that excitement faded over the coming days and weeks as daily events began to retake your attention. Old habits returned and your enthusiasm for higher yields diminished.

Because we forget or can lose focus, we have to set in place a method of reminding ourselves or in other words, nurturing the seeds we've planted. Just as a crop is watered best by a gentle and steady rain, you must be engaged in a daily regiment of bite-sized reminders of the character traits that support your desired harvest. A two hundred bushel per acre life depends on the way you manage each day.

You cannot afford to think that just because you understand something as simple as kindness that you will remember its value when you find yourself in a difficult circumstance. This difficult circumstance could be when it is finally your turn to be waited on at the customer service claim counter when your luggage and business presentation materials did not end up traveling on the same plane that you were on. Planting kindness will in fact help the situation rather than planting discontent but at that very moment you may forget and later regret the way you treated the agent with disrespect.

Vince Lombardi said, "The will to win…The will to achieve…Goes dry without continual reinforcement." The seed of perseverance provides a steadiness to your yield throughout the entire growing process.

The following story has been adapted from the original writings of Elizabeth Silance Ballard. It provides a revealing lesson on the law of the yield and sets the backdrop for further understanding.

FOUR LETTERS FROM TEDDY

There is a story many years ago of an elementary teacher. Her name was Jean Thompson. She stood in front of her fifth-grade class on the very first day of school and told the children that she loved them all the same. But that was impossible because there in the front, slumped in his seat, was a little boy named Teddy Stoddard.

Mrs. Thompson had watched Teddy the year before and noticed that he didn't play well with the other children, that his clothes were messy, and that he constantly needed a bath. Teddy could also be unpleasant. It got to the point where Mrs. Thompson would actually take delight in marking his papers with a broad red pen, making bold Xs and then putting a big F at the top of his papers.

At the school where Mrs. Thompson taught, she was required to review each child's past records, and she put Teddy's off until last. However, when she reviewed his file, she was in for a surprise.

Teddy's first-grade teacher wrote, "Teddy is a bright child with a ready laugh. He does his work neatly and has good manners... He is a joy to be around."

His second-grade teacher wrote, "Teddy is an excellent student, well liked by his classmates, but he is troubled because his mother has a terminal illness and life at home must be a struggle."

His third-grade teacher wrote, "His mother's death has been hard on him. He tries to do his best, but his father doesn't show much interest, and his home life will soon affect him if some steps aren't taken."

Teddy's fourth-grade teacher wrote, "Teddy is withdrawn and doesn't show much interest in school. He doesn't have many friends and sometimes sleeps in class."

By now, Mrs. Thompson realized the problem, and she was ashamed of herself. She felt even worse when her students brought her Christmas presents wrapped in beautiful ribbons and bright paper, except for Teddy's. His present was clumsily wrapped in the heavy, brown paper that he got from a grocery bag. Mrs. Thompson took pains to open it in the middle of the other presents. Some of the children started to laugh when she found a rhinestone bracelet with some of the stones missing and a bottle of perfume that was one-quarter full.

She stifled the children's laughter when she exclaimed how pretty the bracelet was, putting it on, and dabbed some of the perfume on her wrist.

Teddy stayed after school that day just long enough to say, "Mrs. Thompson, today you smelled just like my mom used to."

After the children left, she cried for at least an hour. On that very day, she quit teaching, reading, writing, and arithmetic. Instead, she began to teach children. Mrs. Thompson paid particular attention to Teddy. As she worked with him, his mind seemed to come alive. The more she encouraged him, the faster he responded.

By the end of the year, Teddy had become one of the smartest children in the class, and despite her lie that she would love all the children the same, Teddy became on of her "teacher's pets."

A year later, she found a note under her door, from Teddy, telling her that she was still the best teacher he ever had in his whole life.

Six years went by before she got another note from Teddy. He then wrote that he had finished high school, third in his class, and she was still the best teacher he ever had in his whole life.

Four years after that, she got another letter, saying that while things had been tough at times, he'd stayed in school and would soon graduate from college with the highest honors. He assured Mrs. Thompson that she was still the best and favorite teacher he ever had in his whole life.

Then four more years passed and yet another letter came. This time, he explained that after he got his bachelor's degree, he decided to go a little further. The letter explained that she was still the best and favorite teacher he ever had, but now his name was a little longer. The letter was signed Theodore F. Stoddard, MD.

The story doesn't end there. You see, there was yet another letter that spring. Teddy said he'd met this girl and was going to be married. He explained that his father had died a couple of years ago and he was wondering if Mrs. Thompson might agree to sit in the place at the wedding that was normally reserved for the mother of the groom. Of course, Mrs. Thompson did. And guess what?

She wore that bracelet, the one with several rhinestones missing. And she made sure she was wearing the perfume that Teddy remembered his mother wearing on their last Christmas together. They hugged each other, and Dr. Stoddard whispered in Mrs. Thompson's ear, "Thank you, Mrs. Thompson, for believing in me. Thank you so much for making me feel important and showing me that I could make a difference."

Mrs. Thompson, with tears in her eyes, whispered back, "Teddy, you have it all wrong. You were the one who taught me that I could make a difference. I didn't know how to teach until I met you."

—Found on multiple websites as The Mrs. Thompson Story including www.livinglifefully.com

I believe that Mrs. Thompson became profoundly aware of the fact that she could harvest a greater influence in the lives of her students by the seeds she planted and continued to nurture in her classroom. She became increasingly aware that the seeds she helped plant in the lives of her students could in fact influence their current and future harvest.

Mrs. Thompson further teaches us that the harvest of influence and our ability to make a difference is germinating in every action we perform. Not only was the yield in her own life increased but the yield within the lives of her students increased as well.

This story also teaches us about the seeds that lead to a harvest that will be known as our legacy. What you do to influence the lives of others will continue to improve the yield that is credited to your name.

As you cultivate your character in preparation for planting, you must be willing to acknowledge the areas of your life that need improvement. In your life or organization, you must establish a culture that is conducive to planting. Throwing seeds onto unprepared soil will not yield the desired results.

You must learn from your past, and you must make a plan for improving your future harvest and yield. Long-term planning involves the question, What do I want to harvest five years, ten years and even twenty years from now? Given these desired harvests and yields, you must determine what seeds you need to begin planting today.

John Maxwell once explained the difference between success and significance. He said that success is what we acquire in exchange for our work and effort. Significance is something we acquire when we look beyond ourselves and find ways to share our experience and knowledge with others. One is internal and the other is external.

I believe we all want to be better, do more, and make a difference—in other words, increase our yield. Desire does not stand in our way of becoming better; the problem generally is a lack of time to devote to improving ourselves. We truly are busy, and even though we know it is time well spent, our own self-development often takes a back seat to other demands.

To inspire a student, a teacher must be inspired. To provide excellent patient care, a physician must maintain a compassionate heart. To be a great leader, one must be an effective communicator of their vision and know what inspires others. In other words, in order for you to give your best in any endeavor, you must become your best. When you are continually growing personally, you can 'give' up to your potential. You can increase your yield.

Because your free time is limited, what you must discover is how you can improve your efficiency at uncovering, understanding, and applying the principles that influence your life. You need to find ways to help yourself internalize these principles so that they become a part of your character and thus can automatically be applied to daily events. By utilizing the available resources of discovery, you can improve yourself today and reduce the number of missed opportunities or costly mistakes tomorrow. Each day you can better your previous best.

There are organizations and individuals who have dedicated themselves to exploring, discovering, and documenting specific human behavioral characteristics and professional development skills. There are seminars, books, workbooks, CDs, and DVDs that can accelerate your understanding of a specific skill. There are corporate retreats and in-service meetings that can be devoted to teaching a new skill or to reinforce the importance of existing procedures. It is estimated that there are over one hundred new professional development books published each month.

Availability of information is not the problem. The problem often times is that there is too much information. We see this and ask, What ideas are the most beneficial to me and how can I sift through all of the authors in a timely manner so that the information becomes meaningful, manageable and useful? Being overwhelmed with these choices can legitimately prevent you from knowing how to use these valuable tools and where to even start. The reason many of us don't devote time to ourselves is because it takes too long to sift through all the sand in the river of information to find the golden nuggets.

This is a book about providing solutions. As you continue, we will explore how to accomplish this daily task of living a life with yield in mind.

The things you do when no one is looking are the things that define you.

—Chrysler

To accomplish great things, we must not only act, but also dream; not only plan, but also believe.

—Anatole France

BUILDING A LIFE WITH YIELD IN MIND

I became involved in the building and construction industry somewhat by accident. After completing my degree in business management I worked as a corporate trainer for National Computer Systems (NCS). A few years passed, and I received one of those phone calls you never forget. My mom and dad called to tell me that my dad was diagnosed with cancer and it was inoperable. I resigned from my position with NCS and moved back to Colorado to spend the last months of his life nearby. My life has been different ever since.

I returned to work in the computer industry but also did some moonlighting computer work for a local builder. Within three years, the owner of the company was ready to retire, and I purchased his business. Now, after two decades of owning a residential/light commercial construction business, I continue to realize how similar building a home is to building our lives and organizations. As I mentioned in the Preface, I decided to write this book because I am drawn to do my part in passing along what I have learned and to contribute to the building of people and organizations.

The building process provides a blueprint of how we can build a life with yield in mind.

PRECONSTRUCTION

Often, a client will engage an architect, engineer, and general contractor to help refine their dream and establish a construction budget. This process establishes a master site plan and identifies the scope of work for each facet of construction. At this point, you are building your project on paper.

Similarly, individuals and organizations must have the leadership in place that defines their direction, business philosophy, and business culture. Organizationally, as the owner or key leader, you must provide and successfully communicate your vision of what the company can be. You must understand and define your direction before you can hire the right people with the right skill sets and put them in the right places within the organization.

Individually, you must also decide who you want to be. As arduous as this task can be, it is necessary. Just like a ship without a rudder cannot maintain its course, you must have a clear direction charted, or you will simply wander with no possibility of arriving at any destination. This is a critical component to maximizing organizational and personal yield.

Determine your desired harvest, and identify the seeds that will produce this outcome. Just as a client engages the help of an architect and engineer, you should also seek council from those who care about you and your success.

FINANCING

After you have a clear idea of the project costs, financing becomes the next assignment. A lender helps ensure that the project is feasible from a financial standpoint. They are looking to see if the appraised value supports the cost. Can the client afford the payment? Is the bank at risk if they have to foreclose? Can they liquidate the asset to, at a minimum, reclaim their investment?

Organizationally and individually, you must ask similar questions: Are you willing to invest the time that is necessary to stay the course? Is your direction true to your character and values? As you take a careful appraisal of your plans, is it worth the cost or price you must pay to realize the business and life you are building?

You must know that you are committed and able to be disciplined on this course if you expect to live a two hundred bushel per acre life or realize such a yield in your business. You must make sure you have selected the right seeds and that you have established a plan for nurturing your selected seeds.

CONTINGENCY FUND

Every wise home builder and every good loan program will include a contingency amount to be factored into the loan. A bank may require a 5 percent or 10 percent amount depending on the scope of the project.

In essence, the bank wants to be sure that a reserve fund exists if something on the project does not go as planned. For example, the soil may be more expansive than anticipated, and adjustments must be made in the foundation design. Material costs may fluctuate or weather conditions may add expense.

From a personal and organizational standpoint, you must be prepared for things to not go as planned. Anticipate the need for a contingency plan. One of the most important things I began to understand in both life and business was the difference between my vision and my plan. Your vision generally remains unchanged, but your plan, or how to accomplish your vision, changes or as business climates change.

For example, my vision is to be in a position where I can provide for the financial and physical needs of my family. I went to college with the anticipation that a degree would increase my ability to secure better employment. I was hired by my first employer out of college because of my specific degree. My degree proved to be helpful; however, I realized quickly that this job was not allowing me to fulfill my vision.

Financially, I was unable to afford a large enough home for my growing family. My vision led me to begin looking for a new plan. My vision was right and true, but my plan needed to be improved on a regular basis.

As time passed, I went into business for myself. While I was able to financially provide for my family, the size of my company had grown to the point that I was spending less time at home. My vision was being compromised, and I had to figure out a new plan.

This led me to begin looking for a partner so that I could spend time with my family. In my search for a partner, a buyer for the business came along, and I sold the company.

I was able to distinguish the fact that owning my own business was not my vision. It was just a plan to accomplish my vision. As a part of the sale, I signed a noncompete agreement and committed to stay on board and assist in transitioning in the new management team. I made more money, had more family time and a lot less stress.

After six years, I couldn't recognize the company I had started and sold. The culture had changed, and I needed to change my plan again. My noncompete agreement had expired, so I went back out on my own but much wiser than the first time. I had used my past experience and the experience I had learned from others to create the best plan yet. Fortunately, I was beginning to understand the law of the yield and how it applied to my life and business.

I found one of the keys to success was in not confusing my vision with my plan. My vision remained focused, but I continued to be flexible by always keeping an open mind to a contingency plan.

CONSTRUCTION

Starting the building process after the many months of planning and preparation is an exciting time. It is increasingly exciting and gratifying as you watch each phase of construction from the site excavation, to the concrete being poured, to the framing, to the roofing, to the mechanical systems, to the drywall, to the fixtures being installed and finally to the last brush stoke of paint. There is a process and an order and timing that must be followed. Building requires daily effort and ongoing task management if you expect to realize a completed project.

Building a successful life and organization resembles this same process. Each day – each event – each task – requires your attention and focus. There is an order to planting the right seeds within your character and culture. There is a process that involves continually nurturing those seeds in order to harvest the greatest yield of who you are striving to become personally or organizationally. There is excitement as you see the progress each day of what has been accomplished as well as an excitement about the new seeds you are planting and the anticipation of their future harvest. This is the blueprint to building a happy, fulfilled and productive life.

Now, you must accept the fact that there will be days when specific activities won't go as planned. There are many things out of your control that can compromise your progress. You could experience an equipment failure, a material delivery cancellation, a colleague who is challenging the company culture, a deviation in the economy that directly affects your business or it can simply be a rainy day when you were planning an activity that required sunshine. These things can temporarily challenge your progress but you must remember that the seeds of persistence and focus were planted in your garden so that you could stay true to your vision. Follow your mission statement and be uncompromising in staying true to your values. Don't stop nurturing those good and positive seeds that will produce your desired harvest and maximum yield. As you do, your strength of character will see you through to that last brush stroke of paint.

THE CHANGE ORDER

During construction, it is common that a client will want to integrate a design feature that was not originally considered during the planning process. This change is handled through a Change Order, which documents the details of the change and identifies any cost considerations. If the cost is acceptable to the homebuyer, the change is agreed upon.

Once the Change Order is defined, all associated tradesmen immediately stop what they are doing to meet with the client to discuss the details. The change is often affecting the current construction activities and therefore must immediately be addressed. Time is of the essence so that the project completion schedule is minimally affected.

I believe the Change Order may provide one of the most significant life lessons to be learned from the construction process. When you recognize that something needs to be improved upon in your life or organization, get out a Change Order, and immediately address the details. Don't wait until next fiscal year's planning process or for next year's New Year's resolutions. Make change now!

You need to make change whenever you recognize that your life needs to be built differently. Tear out what is undesirable, and begin building your life or organization the way you really want it to be. Time is of the essence, and it is worth any cost.

I realize that some organizational and personal changes can take time to implement. However, the Change Order process must start immediately upon recognition of the needed change and then be progressively addressed until fully implemented. This will have the greatest impact on your ability to achieve the highest yield in your life.

Through an important event, a young man learned that change was needed in his life. While recalling the time he had spent with his neighbor many years earlier, he came to realize the thing that he needed to value most in his life and business.

THE SMALL GOLD BOX

It had been some time since Jack had seen the old man. College, a young family, career, and life itself got in the way. In fact, Jack moved clear across the country in pursuit of his dreams. There, in the rush of his busy life, Jack had little time to think about the past and often had no time to spend with his wife and son. He was working on his future, and nothing could stop him.

He received a call one evening from his mother. She told him, "Mr. Belser died last night. The funeral is Wednesday."

Memories flashed through his mind like an old newsreel as he sat quietly remembering his childhood days.

"Jack, did you hear me?"

"Oh, sorry, Mom. Yes, I heard you. It's been so long since I thought of him. I'm sorry, but I honestly thought he must have died years ago," Jack said.

"Well, he didn't forget you. Every time I saw him, he'd ask how you were doing. He'd reminisce about the many days you spent over 'his side of the fence' as he put it," his Mom told him.

"I loved that old house he lived in," Jack said.

"You know, Jack, after your father died, Mr. Belser stepped in to make sure you had a man's influence in your life," she said.

"He's the one who taught me carpentry," he said. "I wouldn't be in this business if it weren't for him. He spent a lot of time teaching me things he thought were important... Mom, I'll be there for the funeral," Jack said.

As busy as he was, he kept his word. Jack caught the next flight to his hometown. Mr. Belser's funeral was small and uneventful. He had no children of his own, and most of his relatives had passed away.

The night before he had to return home, Jack and his mom stopped by to see the old house next door one more time.

Standing in the doorway, Jack paused for a moment. It was like crossing over into another dimension, a leap through space and time. The house was exactly as he remembered. Every step held memories. Every picture, every piece of furniture... Jack stopped suddenly.

"What's wrong, Jack?" his mom asked.

"The box is gone," he said

"What box?" Mom asked.

"There was a small gold box that he kept locked on top of his desk. I must have asked him a thousand times what was inside. All he'd ever tell me was 'the thing I value most,'" Jack said.

It was gone. Everything about the house was exactly how Jack remembered it, except for the box. He figured someone from the Belser family had taken it.

"Now I'll never know what was so valuable to him," Jack said. "I better get some sleep. I have an early flight home, Mom."

It had been about two weeks since Mr. Belser died. Returning home from work one day, Jack discovered a note in his mailbox. "Signature required on a package. No one at home. Please stop by the main post office within the next three days," the note read.

Early the next day, Jack retrieved the package. The small box was old and looked like it had been mailed a hundred years ago. The handwriting was difficult to read, but the return address caught his attention. "Mr. Harold Belser," it read.

Jack took the box out to his car and opened the package. There inside was the gold box and an envelope.

Jack's hands shook as he read the note inside. "Upon my death, please forward this box and its contents to

Jack Bennett. It's the thing I valued most in my life."
A small key was taped to the letter. His heart racing, as tears filling his eyes, Jack carefully unlocked the box. There inside he found a beautiful gold pocket watch.

Running his fingers slowly over the finely etched casing, he unlatched the cover.

Inside he found these words engraved:

Jack, thanks for your time! Harold Belser.

"The thing he valued most was...my time"

Jack held the watch for a few minutes, then called his office, and cleared his appointments for the next two days.

"Why?" Janet, his assistant, asked.

"I need some time to spend with my son," he said. "Oh, and by the way, Janet, thanks for your time!"

—Unknown Author Found on multiple websites
including www.lighthouseconsulting.org

———❖———

Use the Change Order in your life when you see yourself heading off course. Immediately, pull any weeds that have crept into your garden and threaten to take nourishment away from the other seeds you've planted. You are the builder of your life, and it requires your immediate attention when you notice that change is needed or when you see a weed that needs to be pulled. Create a personal Change Order form or use the one at the end of this chapter. Identify the area where change is needed, define the new desired harvest, and then plant and nurture the corresponding seeds.

If it is an organizational change for your entire company, communicate your vision of where you want to be. Circulate the Change Order detail, and have everyone sign off and get on board. Then, you must continue to follow through until the change is permanent. Unfortunately, you may find someone who cannot support your new direction. Don't delay making additional changes if needed to support your vision.

When you sacrifice something today for something better tomorrow, the rewards will last a lifetime. Gary Ryan Blair said, "We have to accept that becoming uncomfortable is not a nuisance, but rather a necessity to growth, excellence, and success."

PROJECT COMPLETION

There is a time when the project is complete and ready for occupancy. A Punch List is created for any outstanding items that need fine tuned or adjusted. The final loan disbursements occur, and the keys are turned over to the owner. For the builder, this represents the harvest.

All your labor and commitment up to this point has resulted in a crop that is ready to be brought into the storehouse. In business, in your profession, and in your personal life, this time means that you are realizing some measure of your vision or desired harvest.

There is a moment in time when you feel that you have arrived at your destination. Cooperation is prevalent throughout your organization, you are realizing increased profitability because of increased customer loyalty, or maybe you have developed new and valuable friendships. In general, the seeds you planted are producing your desired harvest and yield.

ONGOING MAINTENANCE

Because of daily use, homeowner maintenance on the property must begin immediately. Touch-up painting may be required to hide a scuff that occurred on a wall while moving furniture into your home. Cleaning the carpet in high traffic areas will be necessary and mechanical systems will demand replacement parts over time. Ongoing care is required to keep everything at its optimal beauty and performance.

To maintain our lives and organizations, you too must engage in the process of ongoing maintenance. The harvest that is now in your storehouse may soon become stale if it is not used or sold. A new growing season is ahead, and you must plant new seeds if you want to continue to have a harvest. If at any point you do not continue to sow the right seeds, your harvest will not be sustained.

The very premise of the law of the yield is based on the fact that the highest yield is a result of ongoing nurturing. As you build a life with yield in mind, you are putting in place the systems that require you to plan, determine the cost, have a contingency plan, be willing to change immediately as needed, recognize and celebrate when you have realized your desired harvest, but then, you must have the fortitude to press forward in order to continually maintain the character traits that support your vision.

These are the key characteristics to building a life with yield in mind.

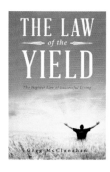

THE LAW OF THE YIELD

THE HIGHEST LAW OF SUCCESSFUL LIVING

CHANGE ORDER

SPECIFY WHAT NEEDS TO BE CHANGED

_____

_____

DESCRIBE YOUR DESIRED HARVEST

_____

_____

_____

IDENTIFY THE SEEDS THAT MUST BE PLANTED

_____   _____

_____   _____

_____   _____

ESTABLISH A NURTURING PLAN

_____

_____

The difference between a successful person and others is not a lack of strength, not a lack of knowledge, but rather a lack in will.

—Vince Lombardi

Never live in the past but always learn from it.

—Anonymous

REARVIEW MIRROR

The rearview mirror was a brilliant and simple idea. Creating a way to have a glimpse at where you have been. I believe there is an important lesson we can learn from the rearview mirror.

A few years ago, I was returning home from a business trip I had made to Albuquerque, New Mexico. As is the case with every summer evening in the southwest, the bugs were out in full force. With every mile I traveled, my windshield became increasingly covered with bug splatter. As luck would have it, I received a direct hit exactly in my line of sight, and for the last 120 miles or so, I had to lean to one side so I could clearly see.

I arrived home late, and the next morning, I got back into my truck and headed into my office. It was only as I drove off in the sunlight that I realized how badly covered my windshield was. My forward view was totally obstructed!

As I maneuvered through traffic, I used my mirrors as needed to navigate from lane to lane. At that point, I realized something interesting. When I looked in my rearview mirror, my view was unobstructed—no bug splatters. I could see clearly behind me.

I guess I was in a reflective mood because it occurred to me how much this resembles our lives. What lies ahead is unpredictable. You never know exactly what's coming. You never know if you will respond to an event or situation in the best way possible. It is only when you look back that you can see clearly just how you may have done something differently—presumably better. The old saying "hindsight is 20/20" rings true.

So here's the question: what can we do today to improve our ability to successfully manage future events?" To have 20/20 vision when looking forward! The best way to improve your yield and to improve it as quickly as possible lies in the answer to this question.

First, you must become an expert at applying your knowledge from past experiences to future events, and secondly, you must be continually engaged in personal and business development opportunities that will allow you to learn from the experiences of others. Let me demonstrate this first idea through the following story.

THE GREAT BALTIMORE FIRE OF 1904

An unknown reporter writes it was a chilly Sunday morning on February 7, 1904. The men of Engine Co. 15 were expecting a quiet day as they readied for inspection. Their routine was interrupted by an automated fire alarm at 10:48 a.m. in the John Hurst and Company building. These men were answering the first call of what would become known as the Great Baltimore Fire of 1904.

Once the fire chief was on the scene, he quickly realized the danger. High winds were causing the blaze to spread quickly and efforts to douse the fire were hampered by the freezing temperatures. He called in nearly the entire Baltimore City Fire Department to fight the fire, but even that was not enough to contain the persistent flames.

A plea for help went out to areas surrounding Baltimore, and the response was astounding. Firefighters from Washington, DC, were the first to arrive. Upon arrival they were dismayed to find out that their fire hose couplings would not fit the fire hydrants. Baltimore, like most cities of that day, had their own standard by which fire hydrants and firefighting equipment were manufactured. As firefighters arrived, they tried to adapt to this different standard but the lowered water pressure and leaks continued to impact their ability to help. Firefighters from as far away as Philadelphia and New York City answered the call, but each time, the story was the same. The lack of a standard caused confusion and the resulting efforts were less effective.

The Great Baltimore Fire raged across the city for two days. Damage caused by the blaze was so extensive that it is hard to imagine. It destroyed over one thousand five hundred buildings covering nearly seventy city blocks.

Congress asked for an investigation of the fire to be conducted in order to determine what may have caused the fire and the reason for its far reaching damages. In a final report submitted to Congress, the lack of a uniform standard was cited as a major contributing factor to the massive destruction. As a result, Congress tasked the National Bureau of Standards now known as the National Institute of Standards and Technology to further investigate the matter. They discovered around six hundred different sizes for fire equipment in use throughout the nation. As a result, the organization established a national standard for fire equipment.

—Wikipedia provided factual details

With this story in mind, you can see that your ability to successfully manage your way through future events can be enhanced by how well you are able to apply your knowledge from past experiences. The establishing of a fire equipment standard didn't fix the problem overnight, but it put the wheels in motion for a universal solution and the hope that this direction would prevent a tragedy of this magnitude from happening again.

Looking behind you for what you can learn from the past is important, *but* the rearview mirror has another valuable lesson that bears consideration. If you measure the size of the rearview mirror in comparison to your windshield, you'll see where you should focus the majority of your attention. On my vehicle, the rearview mirror measures twenty square inches and my windshield measures 1,740 square inches. That means that just over 1 percent of the space is allocated for looking at where I've been.

There is wisdom in this ratio. You should let 1 percent of your thoughts look upon the past for what you can learn, but it is clear that you should not dwell on the past. You can't change it! The good old days are not near as exciting as your future can be! Learn from the past, but make sure that 99 percent of your thoughts are focused on future opportunities and how to adjust your life and business to current market conditions.

For the second stage of learning, you simply must be continually engaged in educational and training opportunities. The saying of "leaders are readers" really is saying "leaders are learners." Take time to learn a new skill, or you may just simply reinforce your understanding of existing skills. This process is critical so that you are able to give your best and realize greater yields more quickly.

In summary, it is through these two ways of learning that you can ensure that you are able to perform at the highest levels of professionalism within your career. This will help you to see 20/20 behind you and improve your forward vision to this same ratio.

To gain strength and clarity, take a few moments, and look in your rearview mirror. Learn what you can, but then it is important to refocus your attention on your future and this year's harvest.

The difference between ordinary and extraordinary is that little extra.

—Jimmie Johnson

THE QUICK RESPONSE AWARD

I think it is safe to assume that all of you have had an experience while purchasing an item where the person that waited on you was an expert in their field and a true professional. They didn't have to check with someone else to answer most, if not all, of your questions. They were able to educate you and assist you in making the best purchase.

I would also imagine that you are familiar with someone who has not paid the price to become an expert and frequently has to ask for assistance from another associate or a member of management. It is clear that for you, your team, or your organization to realize the greatest yield, it must be filled with experts and those who are prepared to fulfill their job duties in the highest level.

At forty-eight years old, I found myself facing open-heart surgery. I was born with a deformed aortic valve, and therefore, I maintained a regiment of periodic visits to my cardiologist. My heart defect (a bicuspid valve) did not cause any restrictions in my activity, and I always felt healthy. However, I had gone in for what I thought would be just another routine echocardiogram, and my cardiologist discovered a tumor inside the aortic chamber of my heart. The actual size of the tumor was not able to be determined so additional tests were ordered.

Smaller rural communities in which I live don't often offer all medical services locally. Cardiovascular surgery is one of those procedures that are referred out of the area. Therefore, within a few days, I was in Phoenix, Arizona, at the St. Joseph's Hospital Heart Institute. It was clear to the doctors that I had a fibroelastoma tumor growing in the aortic chamber of my heart.

Through additional testing, it was determined that surgery was less of a risk than leaving the tumor in my heart. The tumor had grown beyond what they felt was safe as it was large enough that at any moment, a portion of it could break loose, and its next stop would be in my brain.

My wife and I had five days to go home, get things in order, and return for surgery. I have to confess, I spent much more than 1 percent of my thoughts looking in the rearview mirror of my life. I was uncertain of the future, but at the same time, I was so grateful for my past. It is in times like these where the really important things in life become much clearer.

I mentally understood that open-heart surgery is a rather routine operation these days, but this was my heart we were talking about now, not historical statistics. I was aware that there was some risk and that I could be one of those statistics that did not survive the operation. It's probable that I felt more concern because up to this point in my life, I had not had any health issues at all. Even a headache was a rare event.

The four-to five-hour-estimated surgery took nine hours. Things did not go quite as planned. The surgeon found a second tumor, and they replaced my deformed valve with a mechanical valve and also determined that a section of my aortic artery needed replaced. I know it was a very long time for my wife and children to sit and worry. I was told that a nurse came and regularly updated them, but there is always a concern that things are not going well when the surgery takes longer than expected.

After surgery, I was moved to the ICU, and the breathing tube was removed in a few hours. I became partially aware of things shortly thereafter and was experiencing a significant level of pain. The pain predominantly stemmed from the drainage tubes coming out of my chest rather than the incision itself.

I was required to get up and walk the hall with my nurse twice a day. After walking, I experienced increased pain from the movement of the tubes. I would press my Call button, and Matt, my nurse for the first two days, came running. He assessed my pain quickly, and within moments, he was at my bedside, injecting pain medication through my IV.

He knew my file. He knew what I was allowed to be given for pain. He didn't have to check my record or check with the doctor. He was an expert at his job, and he was prepared to offer the highest level of patient care.

After a few days, I was moved to the seventh floor of the Heart and Lung Tower at the hospital. I received the greatest of patient care at all levels. The first few nights while my drainage tubes were still in place, I continued to experience excruciatingly painful nights. I pressed my Call button, and Brooke came running. She too knew my chart and knew what I was able to receive to stabilize the pain. She ran out and ran back in order to get me relief as fast as she could.

As I lay awake in my bed on the fifth night after surgery, hoping the final drainage tube would come out the following day, I thought about how impressed I was specifically with Matt and Brooke's quick response on my behalf. As I considered what made them different, it was their familiarity with everything about my records and their level of skill. These two things combined put them in a position that they could provide excellent care. They had also planted the right seeds within their character that made them caring and compassionate. They exemplify two individuals that understood the principles associated with the law of the yield.

The Quick Response Award is a way of awarding those that exemplify excellence in their life and career. Wise leaders and organizations are those that have the right people in the right places with the right training to improve the yield of the entire organization. These are the organizations that trust their employees to make decisions because they have given them the proper training and have tested their character over time.

To be the company that thrives in the marketplace when your competitor is struggling to make ends meet, you would not have to look much further than to the level of expertise that prevails throughout each organization. If you cannot hand out The Quick Response Award to each key staff member, you're giving your competitor the opportunity to earn a greater percentage of the market share. You must help your team members to continually plant the personal seeds of greatness that will help them perform at their highest level. Your success—your highest yield as an organization—hangs in the balance.

As an employee, your job security improves in direct proportion to your ability to become an expert in your field but also in your ability to plant the seeds necessary for you to maximize your level of professionalism.

As a brief tribute, I have the utmost respect and praise for Dr. Brian de Guzman as he had the endurance to stand over me and work with such precision on my heart for nine hours. The thing that means the most is that he had paid the price to become an expert, and his expertise saved my life. Not only is he a skilled surgeon, but equally important, he is the kind of individual that took a personal interest in me and my family. He knew that living a life of yield was much more than just having the answers and skill, but it also meant he was someone you would enjoy having as a friend.

You can see that yield is not just found in your skill, but it also includes every area of your character. This combination will qualify you for The Quick Response Award.

The road to success is always under construction.

—Lily Tomlin

Your job should not define you but the way you do your job reveals who you are.

—Nathan Mellor

YIELD IN ACTION

I have accumulated hundreds of stories over my lifetime. There are many great stories of others that have taught me valuable lessons about how to live at a higher level. Being able to accomplish a greater yield in your life will come more quickly if you can accelerate your growth by learning from other's positive examples. To me, many of these stories represent a type of modern-day parable.

I agree with the Indian Proverb, which states,

> Tell me a fact and I'll learn; tell me a truth and I'll believe, but tell me a story and it will live in my heart forever.

In this chapter I provide twenty-five stories of individuals caught in the act of greatness. Each story represents a key topic that, when implemented into your life, will increase your yield. Some of these stories you may have already heard, but like the story of "A Christmas Carol," there is something every year that Mr. Scrooge reminds us about. We rediscover the wonderful reward of doing something for others, and that to get, you must give.

It is my hope that the same emotion I feel through these stories will also influence your life and that the message of each story can live in your heart forever. As I mentioned earlier, your ability to achieve the highest levels of yield will be shortened if you can not only learn from your own experiences but if you can also learn from the example of others. If you want to improve your yield, you must put yourself and your organization in a position where you are engaged in inspiring and motivating training on a regular basis.

Reasonable effort has been made to find the original author's of these stories and acknowledge them as such. I feel badly that in many cases, the author is unknown and proper credit and recognition cannot be made. I appreciate the way their words have stirred my soul and made me better.

You may choose to use each of the following messages as a personal or staff development topic for an entire week. Plant each topic, nourish it, water it throughout the week, and see how it can assist you in your life and organization. Continue to explore other supporting content that can further nurture each character trait. Refer back to these stories frequently in conversation so that the principles being taught will continue to live in your heart and become a part of the culture of your organization.

I strongly encourage you to make frequent visits to www.lawoftheyield.com for additional supporting content. Here you will find inspirational videos from The Foundation for a Better Life and many other wonderful resources. These video clips greatly enhance each topic as you participate in these visual presentations. Additional resources will continue to be added to the website in order to continually nurture your understanding and application of each topic.

YIELD IN ACTION NUMBER 1

FOCUS

An important part of building a life with yield in mind is staying focused. I'd been thinking about the importance of focus when I came across this story. We become so busy at times that we can be distracted doing good things and fail to focus on the best things. If you want to realize the highest levels of yield in your life, it is imperative that you maintain your focus and to make sure that you focus on the best things. In the video presentation created by The Foundation for a Better Life and available through www.lawoftheyield.com, you will see a father who readily helped others. He was a good man, and I am sure enjoyed helping others, but I believe he was predominantly focused on teaching his son how to live.

You will also see in this video, a young boy who knew just where to focus the light so his father could see—all the while learning without realizing who he was becoming. Both of them accomplished great things by maintaining their focus. We need to learn to apply these same principles in our life and career. The seed of focus is imperative to living a life with yield in mind.

Below is a story that further demonstrates this point. Here we find another father whose focus made all the difference in his son's life. Through a seemingly small daily habit, this father was able to find a way to pay for his son's college and give him the chance at a better life.

The Pickle Jar

As far back as I can remember, the pickle jar sat on the floor beside the dresser in my parents' bedroom. When my father got ready for bed, he would empty his pockets and toss his coins into the jar.

As a small boy, I was always fascinated at the sounds the coins made as they were dropped into the jar. They ended with a merry jingle when the jar was almost empty. Then the tones gradually muted to a dull thud as the jar was filled. I used to squat on the floor in front of the jar and admire the copper and silver circles that glinted like a pirate's treasure when the sun poured through the bedroom window.

When the jar was filled, Dad would sit at the kitchen table and roll the coins before taking them to the bank. Taking the coins to the bank was always a big production. Stacked neatly in a small cardboard box, the coins were placed between Dad and me on the seat of his old truck. Each and every time, as we drove to the bank, Dad would look at me hopefully.

"Those coins are going to keep you out of the textile mill, son. You're going to do better than me. This old mill town's not going to hold you back."

Each and every time, as he slid the box of rolled coins across the counter at the bank toward the cashier, he would grin proudly.

"These are for my son's college fund. He'll never work at the mill all his life like me."

We would always celebrate each deposit by stopping for an ice cream cone. I always got chocolate. Dad always got vanilla. When the clerk at the ice cream parlor handed Dad his change, he would show me the few coins nestled in his palm.

"When we get home, we'll start filling the jar again."

He always let me drop the first coins into the empty jar. As they rattled around with a brief, happy jingle, we grinned at each other.

"You'll get to college on pennies, nickels, dimes, and quarters," he said. "But you'll get there. I'll see to that."

The years passed, and I finished college and took a job in another town. Once, while visiting my parents, I used the phone in their bedroom and noticed that the pickle jar was gone. It had served its purpose and had been removed. A lump rose in my throat as I stared at the spot beside the dresser where the jar had always stood. My dad was a man of few words and never lectured me on the values of determination, perseverance, and faith. The pickle jar had taught me all these virtues far more eloquently than the most flowery of words could have done.

When I married, I told my wife, Susan, about the significant part the lowly pickle jar had played in my life as a boy. In my mind, it defined, more than anything else, how much my dad had loved me. No matter how rough things got at home, Dad continued to doggedly drop his coins into the jar. Even the summer when Dad got laid off from the mill and Mama had to serve dried beans several times a week, not a single dime was taken from the jar.

To the contrary, as Dad looked across the table at me pouring ketchup over my beans to make them more palatable, he became more determined than ever to make a way out for me.

"When you finish college, son," he told me with glistening eyes, "you'll never have to eat beans again... unless you want to."

The first Christmas after our daughter, Jessica, was born, we spent the holiday with my parents. After dinner, Mom and Dad sat next to each other on the sofa, taking turns cuddling their first grandchild. Jessica began to whimper softly, and Susan took her from Dad's arms.

"She probably needs to be changed," she said.

Susan carried her into my parents' bedroom to diaper her. When Susan came back into the living room, there was a strange mist in her eyes. She handed Jessica back to Dad before taking my hand and leading me into the room.

"Look," she said softly, her eyes directing me to a spot on the floor beside the dresser. To my amazement, there, as if it had never been removed, stood the old pickle jar. The bottom was already covered with coins. I walked over to the pickle jar, dug down into my pocket, and pulled out a fistful of coins.

With a gamut of emotions choking me, I dropped the coins into the jar. I looked up and saw that Dad, carrying Jessica, had slipped quietly into the room. Our eyes locked, and I knew he was feeling the same emotions I felt.

Neither one of us could speak as the tears readily flowed.

—Unknown Author Found on multiple
websites including www.inspire21.com

AUTHOR'S INSIGHTS

Seeds that were planted: love, sacrifice, commitment, service, integrity, caring, vision, and focus

Associated harvest: character, realization of dreams, and legacy

The yield is achievement and is found in the lives of those who stay focused.

Love can be the greatest power in driving us to focus on the best things we can do each day. Your love for your family and my love for mine make it easy for us to make sacrifices as we stay focused on the things we can accomplish on their behalf. As you go to work each day, realize that you must strive to serve each client or colleague that walks in your door by focusing on their needs and circumstances. Carry an attitude of hope. Be hopeful that all the while as you work that you can make a difference in their lives.

Clients know if your focus is on them by your actions and conversation. They know, for example, if you are focused on them or focused on your commission and profits. Change your focus or the seeds you are planting, and your profits will soar as a natural harvest.

If the father in the story were to have focused on his bills and household expenses or if he were to have focused on the things he wanted to buy for himself, the pickle jar would have been empty. It is when we focus on the right things that we are able to accomplish great things.

One very important point is to realize that your ability and willingness to remain focused can absolutely make up for a lack of ability. Aesop's fable about the race between "The Tortoise and the Hare" makes this point very clear. The race is not always won by the strongest or fastest but rather victory often goes to the one who remains focused.

I encourage you to focus your devotion and attention on the right seeds that will allow you to realize your greatest harvest and greatest yield.

YIELD IN ACTION NUMBER 2

SERVICE AND RECOGNIZING OTHER'S NEEDS

The following story was written by Maureen Nunn. It tells of a time in her family's life that helps us discover that we are rich through what we give and that there are times when all of us might need a little help.

A Rare Mongolian Rabbit

Perhaps the frequency with which it so often happens nowadays should have lessened the pain; misery does love company after all, but hearing that my husband's job would be "phased out" was unforgettable and shocking.

John, my husband of ten years, expressed his concern over the nightmare occurrence. He assured me that he would do everything possible to get a job to provide for our family. With three children under the age of five and one due very shortly, we relied on his income entirely.

"Life goes on," John said, more outwardly upbeat than I over the situation. "We have our health, and after all, it's only a job. Besides, the company will continue paying me for three more months. I'll surely have a new job by then. Just relax and don't worry."

With his excellent university and professional credentials, I figured he must be right. He was a former Olympic athlete and knew about taking on a challenge. His father died when John was young, so he took on the responsibility of keeping his mother, sister, and brothers together. My husband knew how to work hard and smart. But as the months passed and no job possibilities materialized for him, I grew more and more fearful. What if he couldn't find a job? Under other circumstances could I have returned to classroom teaching, but our fourth child was due in less than three months.

With little money in our savings account, the mortgage payment two months behind, and no possible income from any other source, I whittled away at our daily living budget.

Eventually, our food budget became almost nonexistent. One day while in the supermarket with my children, I noticed a young box boy packing overly ripe fruit and outdated food into cardboard boxes. Hesitantly, I inquired about the destination of the food. "We sell it real cheap, and whatever isn't sold is thrown away," he said. I eyed the aging carrots, celery, and tomatoes. Food we could use for weeks. What, I wondered, is the proper etiquette for begging for food for one's children?

"We have a rare Mongolian rabbit!" I heard myself blurt out, glancing at my three hungry children. "I'd be interested in purchasing the food for the rabbit."

He replied easily, "Since it's just a rabbit, there won't be any charge."

That day he loaded five boxes of produce into my car. We talked while he worked, me sharing information about my soon-to-be expanding family and him talking about his. His name was Jeff. I learned he came from a family of five where finances were tight. This job helped pay for his college education.

Weeks went by, and Jeff began packing the boxes with outdated or damaged items—peanut butter, soup, and cheese—that were otherwise still good but would be thrown away. "Surely a rare rabbit would eat all these items," he said, explaining their inclusion. As the weeks turned into months, we discovered, hidden under the produce, laundry detergent, milk, juice, butter... The list goes on and on.

Jeff started phoning me every time he had a box of "rabbit food" ready. Now and then, he brought the boxes to our home. He never inquired after the rabbit, content instead to leave its food and be on his way.

When our fourth daughter was born, my elation was tinged with worry about our financial future. However, as fate would have it, my husband slipped into the hospital room and said, "I have good news and sad news. The good news is that this morning, I've been offered a very exciting job." I closed my eyes with deep gratitude in my heart. "The sad news," he continued, "is that the rare Mongolian rabbit is gone."

It turned out Jeff no longer worked at the supermarket. While I'd been busy with the birth of our new baby, he had moved, the manager said, and left no forwarding address.

Over the next ten years, I made good on a silent promise I had made to repay the kindness of all who had helped us throughout that difficult time. But my thanks were incomplete. Then one day, a decade later, there was Jeff standing in the store's office. I noticed the title of Manager on his name badge.

How does one adequately thank the person who offers assistance without compromising you pride, extends a hand without sapping your strength, and believes in the rare Mongolian rabbits hiding somewhere in each of our lives? I'm not surprised Jeff's risen up the ranks. He has a rare gift. He knew how to listen loudly to my special plea.

"Mrs. Nunn!" he exclaimed. "I think of you and your family often. How is the rabbit?" he inquired softly.

Taking Jeff's hands into mine, I whispered with a wink, "Thanks for asking. The rabbit moved on long ago, and we couldn't be better."

—Written by Maureen Nunn, excerpted from Kay Allenbaugh's "Chocolate for a Mother's Heart".

AUTHOR'S INSIGHTS

Seeds that were planted: compassion, understanding, caring, and responsiveness

Associated harvest: love, respect, appreciation, friendship, and promotion

The yield is the ability to recognize others needs and a willingness to offer meaningful service.

John Lubbock said, "What we see depends mainly on what we look for."

I encourage you to see what others may quietly be asking for help with under the camouflage of a rare rabbit. When it comes to your family or those around you, if you are looking, you will see if there are special needs and then — caring action can be taken. This is one of the hallmarks possessed by those who live a life of yield.

YIELD IN ACTION NUMBER 3

UNDERSTANDING AND GIVING BACK

It is incredibly rewarding when we can find a way to give back to someone who has helped us in the past. It is rewarding to help anyone in need, but there is something special about "returning the favor." As you will read, something marvelous happens to everyone involved when giving, with no expected reward, takes place.

A Thanks "Giving" Meal

The man slowly looked up. This was a woman clearly accustomed to the finer things of life. Her coat was new. She looked like she had never missed a meal in her life. His first thought was that she wanted to make fun of him, like so many others had done before.

"Leave me alone," he growled. To his amazement, the woman continued standing. She was smiling, her white teeth displayed in dazzling rows.

"Are you hungry?" she asked.

"No," he answered sarcastically. "I've just come from dining with the president. Now go away."

The woman's smile became even broader.

Suddenly, the man felt a gentle hand under his arm. "What are you doing, lady?" the man asked angrily. "I said to leave me alone."

Just then, a policeman came up. "Is there a problem, ma'am?" he asked.

"No problem here, Officer," the woman answered. "I'm just trying to get this man to his feet. Will you help me?"

The officer scratched his head. "That's old Jack. He's been a fixture around here for a couple of years. What do you want with him?"

"See that cafeteria over there?" she asked. "I'm going to get him something to eat and get him out of the cold for a while."

"Are you crazy, lady?" the homeless man resisted. "I don't want to go in there!" Then he felt strong hands grab his other arm and lift him up.

"Let me go, Officer. I didn't do anything."

"This is a good deal for you, Jack," the officer answered. "Don't blow it."

Finally, and with some difficulty, the woman and the police officer got Jack into the cafeteria and sat him at a table in a remote corner. It was the middle of the morning, so most of the breakfast crowd had already left and the lunch bunch had not yet arrived.

The manager strode across the cafeteria and stood by his table.

"What's going on here, Officer?" he asked. "What is all this? Is this man in trouble?"

"This lady brought this man in here to be fed," the policeman answered.

"Not in here!" the manager replied angrily. "Having a person like that here is bad for business."

Old Jack smiled a toothless grin. "See, lady. I told you so. Now if you'll let me go. I didn't want to come here in the first place"

The woman turned to the cafeteria manager and smiled. "Sir, are you familiar with Eddy and Associates, the banking firm down the street?"

"Of course I am," the manager answered impatiently. "They hold their weekly meetings in one of my banquet rooms."

"And do you make a goodly amount of money providing food at these weekly meetings?"

"What business is that of yours?"

"I, sir, am Penelope Eddy, president and CEO of the company."

"Oh…"

The woman smiled again. "I thought that might make a difference." She glanced at the policeman who was busy stifling a laugh. "Would you like to join us in a cup of coffee and a meal, Officer?"

"No thanks, ma'am," the officer replied. "I'm on duty."

"Then, perhaps, a cup of coffee to go?"

"Yes, ma'am. That would be very nice."

The cafeteria manager turned on his heel. "I'll get your coffee for you right away, Officer."

The officer watched him walk away. "You certainly put him in his place," he said.

"That was not my intent. Believe it or not, I have a reason for all this."

She sat down at the table across from her amazed dinner guest. She stared at him intently.

"Jack, do you remember me?"

Old Jack searched her face with his old, rheumy eyes. "I think so... I mean, you do look familiar."

"I'm a little older perhaps," she said "Maybe I've even filled out more than in my younger days when you worked here, and I came through that very door, cold and hungry."

"Ma'am?" the officer said questioningly. He couldn't believe that such a magnificently turned out woman could ever have been hungry.

"I was just out of college," the woman began. "I had come to the city looking for a job, but I couldn't find anything. Finally, I was down to my last few cents and had been kicked out of my apartment. I walked the streets for days. It was February, and I was cold and nearly starving. I saw this place and walked in on the off chance that I could get something to eat."

Jack lit up with a smile. "Now I remember," he said. "I was behind the serving counter. You came up and asked me if you could work for something to eat. I said that it was against company policy."

"I know," the woman continued. "Then you made me the biggest roast beef sandwich that I had ever seen, gave me a cup of coffee, and told me to go over to a corner table and enjoy it. I was afraid that you would get into trouble. Then, when I looked over and saw you put the price of my food in the cash register, I knew then that everything would be all right."

"So you started your own business?" Old Jack said.

"I got a job that very afternoon. I worked my way up. Eventually, I started my own business." She opened her purse and pulled out a business card. "When you are finished here, I want you to pay a visit to a Mr. Lyons. He's the personnel director of my company. I'll go talk to him now, and I'm certain he'll find something for you to do around the office."

She smiled. "I think he might even find the funds to give you a little advance so that you can buy some clothes and get a place to live until you get on your feet. If you ever need anything, my door is always open to you."

There were tears in the old man's eyes. "How can I ever thank you?" he asked.

"Don't thank me," the woman answered. "I am just returning the favor you once showed to me."

Outside the cafeteria, the officer and the woman paused at the entrance before going their separate ways.

"Thank you for all your help, Officer," she said.

"On the contrary, Ms. Eddy," he answered. "Thank you. I saw a miracle today, something that I will never forget."

—Unknown Author Found on multiple websites including www.helpothers.org

AUTHOR'S INSIGHTS

Seeds that were planted: loyalty, friendship, compassion, generosity, kindness, and understanding

Associated harvest: integrity, charity, love, and respect

The yield is the ability to understand others needs and a desire to be of service.

We have opportunities all around us to give of ourselves. Generosity may be the most important trait in building a life filled with yield, meaning, and success. Look for those moments when an unsuspecting spouse, family member, friend, customer, business associate, or a complete stranger can be touched by your generosity.

Remember the words of Sir Winston Churchill:

We make a living by what we get,
but we make a life by what we give.

YIELD IN ACTION NUMBER 4

COMPASSION

I love sports stories—especially the ones that won't make the ESPN headlines. It is on the field of play that you can often find people being caught in the act of goodness. In this story, ESPN's Rick Riley reports that there are some games when cheering for the other side feels better than winning.

Cheering for the Other Side

They played the strangest game in high school football history last month down in Grapevine, Texas.

It was Grapevine Faith versus Gainesville State School, and everything about it was upside down. For instance, when Gainesville came out to take the field, the Faith fans made a forty-yard spirit line for them to run through.

Did you hear that? The other team's fans?

They even made a banner for players to crash through at the end. It said, "Go Tornadoes!" Which is also weird because Faith are the Lions.

It was rivers running uphill and cats petting dogs. More than two hundred Faith fans sat on the Gainesville side and kept cheering the Gainesville players on by name.

"I never in my life thought I'd hear people cheering for us to hit their kids," recalls Gainesville's QB and middle linebacker, Isaiah. "I wouldn't expect another

104

parent to tell somebody to hit their kids. But they wanted us to!"

And even though Faith walloped them 33–14, the Gainesville kids were so happy that after the game, they gave their head coach, Mark Williams, a sideline squirt-bottle shower like he'd just won state. Gotta be the first Gatorade bath in history for an 0–9 coach.

But then you saw the twelve uniformed officers escorting the fourteen Gainesville players off the field. They lined the players up in groups of five—handcuffs ready in their back pockets—and marched them to the team bus. That's because Gainesville is a maximum-security correctional facility seventy-five miles north of Dallas. Every game it plays is on the road.

This all started when Faith's head coach, Kris Hogan, wanted to do something kind for the Gainesville team. Faith had never played Gainesville, but he already knew the score. After all, Faith was 7–2 going into the game, Gainesville 0–8 with two touchdowns all year. Faith has seventy kids, eleven coaches, the latest equipment and involved parents. Gainesville has a lot of kids with convictions for drugs, assault, and robbery—many of whose families had disowned them—wearing seven-year-old pads and ancient helmets.

So Hogan had this idea. What if half our fans—for one night only—cheered for the other team? He sent out an e-mail asking the parents to do just that. "Here's the message I want you to send." Hogan wrote. "You are just as valuable as any other person on planet earth."

Some people were naturally confused. One Faith player walked into Hogan's office and asked, "Coach, why are we doing this?"

And Hogan said, "Imagine if you didn't have a home life. Imagine if everybody had pretty much given up on you. Now imagine what it would mean for hundreds of people to suddenly believe in you."

Next thing you know, the Gainesville Tornadoes were turning around on their bench to see something they never had before. Hundreds of fans. And actual cheerleaders!

"I thought maybe they were confused," said Alex, a Gainesville lineman (only first names are released by the prison). "They started yelling 'Defense!' when their team had the ball. I said, 'What? Why they cheerin' for us?'"

It was a strange experience for boys who most people cross the street to avoid. "We can tell people are a little afraid of us when we come to the games," said Gerald, a lineman who will wind up doing more than three years. "You can see it in their eyes. They're lookin' at us like we're criminals. But these people, they were yellin' for us! By our names!"

Maybe it figures that Gainesville played better than it had all season, scoring the game's last two touchdowns. Of course, this might be because Hogan put his third-string nose guard at safety and his third-string cornerback at defensive end. Still...

After the game, both teams gathered in the middle of the field and that's when Isaiah surprised everybody by saying, "I don't know how this happened, so I don't know how to say thank you, but I never would've known there was so many people in the world that cared about us."

As the Tornadoes walked back to their bus under guard, they each were handed a bag for the ride home—a burger, some fries, a soda, some candy, and an encouraging letter from a Faith player.

The Gainesville coach saw Hogan, grabbed him hard by the shoulders, and said, "You'll never know what your people did for these kids tonight. You'll never, ever know."

And as the bus pulled away, all the Gainesville players crammed to one side and pressed their hands to the window, staring at these people they'd never met before, watching their waves and smiles disappearing into the night.

It's nice to know that one of the best things you can give is still absolutely free.

Hope.

—Rick Reilly, *ESPN the Magazine*

AUTHOR'S INSIGHTS

Seeds that were planted: compassion, faith, example, and leadership

Associated harvest: hope, admiration, respect, love, and encouragement

The yield is a realization that your encouragement and compassion will make a difference in others lives.

Staying the course in our lives is of paramount importance. Each new day, be a positive influence around your customers, colleagues, family, friends, or a complete stranger. When you do, you'll look back and realize your growth and how your goodness has spilled out of your life everywhere you've traveled.

The byproduct of finding ways to give of yourself is that you will achieve the admiration of those around you. This truly will be a measure of living a life with yield in mind.

YIELD IN ACTION NUMBER 5

EFFORT AND THE EXTRA MILE

You will be well served to continually strive to find ways to drive the "extra mile." From seemingly small tasks to great moments, you can quietly have a positive influence on every situation. As you will read in the following, a cab driver made all the difference in the world to one passenger because he was willing to take a road less traveled.

The Cab Ride

Under these circumstances, many drivers would have just honked once or twice, waited a minute, and then driven away. But I had seen too many impoverished people who depended on taxis as their only means of transportation. Unless a situation smelled of danger,

I always went to the door. This passenger might be someone who needs my assistance, I reasoned to myself.

So I walked to the door and knocked. "Just a minute," answered a frail, elderly voice. I could hear something being dragged across the floor. After a long pause, the door opened. A small woman in her nineties stood before me. She was wearing a print dress and a pillbox hat with a veil pinned on it, like somebody out of a 1940s movie.

By her side was a small nylon suitcase. The apartment looked as if no one had lived in it for years. All the furniture was covered with sheets. There were no clocks on the walls, no knickknacks or utensils on the counters. In the corner was a cardboard box filled with photos and glassware.

"Would you please carry my bag out to the car?" she said.

I took the suitcase to the cab and then returned to assist the woman.

She took my arm, and we walked slowly toward the curb. She kept thanking me for my kindness. "It's nothing," I told her. "I just try to treat my passengers the way I would want my mother treated."

"Oh, you're such a good boy," she said.

When we got in the cab, she gave me an address and then asked, "Could you drive through downtown?"

"It's not the shortest way," I answered quickly.

"Oh, I don't mind," she said. "I'm in no hurry. I'm on my way to a hospice."

I looked in the rearview mirror. Her eyes were glistening. "I don't have any family left," she continued. "The doctor says I don't have very long."

I quietly reached over and shut off the meter.

"What route would you like me to take?" I asked.

For the next two hours, we drove through the city. She showed me the building where she had once worked as an elevator operator. We drove through the neighborhood where she and her husband had lived when they were newlyweds. She had me pull up in front of a furniture warehouse that had once been a ballroom where she had gone dancing as a girl.

Sometimes she'd ask me to slow in front of a particular building or corner and would sit staring into the darkness, saying nothing.

As the first hint of sun was creasing the horizon, she suddenly said, "I'm tired. Let's go now."

We drove in silence to the address she had given me. It was a low building, like a small convalescent home, with a driveway that passed under a portico. Two orderlies came out to the cab as soon as we pulled up. They were solicitous and intent, watching her every move. They must have been expecting her.

I opened the trunk and took the small suitcase to the door. The woman was already seated in a wheelchair.

"How much do I owe you?" she asked, reaching into her purse.

"Nothing," I said.

"You have to make a living," she answered.

"There are other passengers," I responded.

Almost without thinking, I bent over and gave her a hug. She held on to me tightly.

"You gave an old woman a little moment of joy," she said. "Thank you."

I squeezed her hand and then walked into the dim morning light. Behind me, a door shut. It was the sound of the closing of a life.

I didn't pick up any more passengers that shift. I drove aimlessly lost in thought. For the rest of that day, I could hardly talk. What if that woman had gotten an angry driver or one who was impatient to end his shift?

What if I had refused to take the run or had honked once and driven away?

On a quick review, I don't think that I have done anything more important in my life.

—Kent Nerburn from *Make Me An Instrument of Your Peace*

AUTHOR'S INSIGHTS

Seeds that were planted: compassion, extra effort, goodness, duty, and service

Associated harvest: appreciation, understanding, awareness, and love

The yield is an understanding of how the smallest acts of kindness are appreciated by others and can make all the difference.

We are conditioned to think that our lives revolve around great moments. But great moments often catch us unaware, beautifully wrapped in what others may consider a small one. One of the keys to your success is in being able to create memorable moments in the small things you do for those around you. If you will just pause for a few seconds and evaluate each situation you are facing, you will be able to see which route you should drive for others. Remember this story, and realize that it is seldom the shortest distance when you go the extra mile, but it is always worth it!

YIELD IN ACTION NUMBER 6
STRENGTH OF CHARACTER

I'd like to share my favorite baseball story. If you don't follow baseball, don't worry. It isn't really about the game of baseball.

I find that the human will is the one thing that has triumphed against unbelievable odds. Successful people all have this universal strength of character. As you will read in this story, sometimes that human will needs a little nudge to put it in motion. You can carry a torch that allows you to see through the darkness and know when a family member, colleague, or a client might need your encouragement. Step up to the plate. You'll be surprised how often you hit it out of the park.

Thanks, Joe

"Beer, getcha ice-cold beer," echoed through Yankee Stadium. Peanuts, popcorn, and a zillion other smells wafted over the warm summer breeze as the crowd roared expectantly.

There was the man—long, lean Joltin' Joe DiMaggio—coming up to the plate, an unlikely hero for a little girl. Yet the Yankee Clipper went on to gain top spot in my personal Hall of Fame.

Years later, our fourteen-year-old son, Larry, made honor roll, became a hometown baseball star, and started avidly collecting baseball trivia. The sport ruled his life, and everyone just knew this kid would make it to the majors. No doubt about it.

We were a baseball family back then. Three or four evenings a week, plus weekends, we'd all rush through an early dinner and head out to the ballpark for games or practice.

Larry cheerfully took a job that summer that would help him reach another goal—buying a ten-speed bike. In spite of my concerns, he turned on his smiling charm and convinced me that our Connecticut hills required all those speeds. As usual with this lovable kid, I caved. He seemed so strong—so indestructible.

One afternoon, Larry took off on his beloved new bike for a quick swim before going to work. He never took that swim. He never arrived at work.

Coming down a hilly, curvy road, Larry and the bike hit a pile of sand. The bike stopped. Larry didn't. He sailed through the air, plummeted down a ravine, and hit a tree trunk—with his face.

Larry broke every bone in his skull, as well as most bones in his face. Helmets for cyclists were unheard of back then.

A month or so later, after several surgeries, including a craniotomy, my son came home. He walked into the house—a tall, bald, and disfigured skeleton went into his room and shut the door.

Our family's collective heart broke as the days and weeks went by. Other than visits to various doctors, Larry never ventured out. He didn't allow his friends in. It seemed as though his spirit had died.

The neurosurgeon told Larry, "No more contact sports, son, other than baseball, that is." Horrified that he would encourage my son to more risk, I questioned his reasoning. The doctor wisely explained, "While playing ball might be dangerous for Larry, to take away that part of his life could be worse."

As the months passed, I found myself wanting him to play ball, as box by box and folder by folder, Larry's baseball treasures came out of his room. "Throw these away," he'd mumble through wired jaws. "I don't want them anymore."

Late one afternoon, a close neighbor came by to see our reclusive son. As the father of his best friend, Russ was allowed into his increasingly private sanctuary. A short while later, Larry came bounding down the hall. "Mom! Dad!" he called excitedly. "Look at this, will ya?"

He held up a large autographed photograph of Joe DiMaggio. "I'm gonna show this to Jimmy and Mike." With that, he dashed out of the house and ran over the hill to find his buddies—for the first time in months.

Bewildered and amazed at the sudden turn of events, I couldn't wait to hear what had happened. We sat down as Russ, a private jet pilot for a business magnate, explained his latest flight. His only passenger that day had turned out to be Joe DiMaggio.

During the flight, Russ told the famous center fielder all about our son. After landing and while still on the tarmac, Joe stopped, opened his briefcase, took out a photograph of himself, and inscribed, "Hang in there, kid, you can do it," and handed it over to Russ. Russ watched a single tear roll down Joe's face.

One compassionate droplet for an unknown boy's hopes and dreams—just one moment in a famous athlete's busy life—generated a glorious rebirth for our son.

Once out of his shell, Larry went on to play baseball, attend college, and marry. He now has children of his own. The photograph of Joe still hangs in Larry's bedroom wall and smiles down at him every night. Every night, Larry smiles back.

—Written by Lynn Layton Zielinski,
excerpted from Kay Allenbaugh's
"Chocolate for a Mother's Heart."

AUTHOR'S INSIGHTS

Seeds that were planted: time, hope, meaning, compassion, and encouragement

Associated harvest: miracles, happiness, appreciation, and respect

The yield is an awareness that our greatest strength and accomplishments stem from our strength of character.

I hope you realize that every day, you are able to positively influence the lives of those around you. This equally applies to the workplace with your colleagues and clients. Imagine if everyone in your office lived by the simple motto of providing encouragement to each other. Imagine if expressions of appreciation made up the discussions at the water cooler. Imagine what would happen when your clients sense a spirit of cooperation and respect throughout your organization.

Sales is a transference of feeling. If you want to improve sales, focus on the climate and culture of your office. The byproduct will be a higher conversion percentage of prospects to buyers. Too many organizations focus on sales volume and quotas rather than in developing the human factor and climate within their organization. It is my experience that the reverse will in fact produce a greater yield.

YIELD IN ACTION NUMBER 7
LOVE

Kenneth Parsons said, "The gift of love is about the only present that isn't exchanged after Christmas."

A story that I turn to each Christmas season tells about a boy named Jerry and describes the love he had for his big brother. It is a remarkable story that provides an example I will always strive to emulate.

Our capacity to love is not based on our intellect nor can we earn a degree in this subject and proudly display such a diploma on our wall. It is developed on the inside and is the most significant character trait that we can possess. As you will read, love is Jerry.

The Gift

I remember it was the same year my father had lost his job. He couldn't find one for a long time, and I remember the burning candles at home because the electricity had been turned off. Even my only sweater had holes and my socks resembled Swiss cheese. We had never really been poor, but the hurdles of the past year had left us quite bad off. The neighbors had offered help, but Dad was proud and refused their offers of help. He told them we'd make out okay.

I couldn't understand the whole situation, but it seemed to me that my younger brother, Jerry, who had mowed lawns all summer long owned 80 percent of our family wealth. He kept his money in a big piggy bank on top of his dresser drawers. Every once in a while, I'd sneak in and grab a little but only when I had a worthy cause. I mean, he couldn't exactly be saving for college, not in his condition he wasn't.

You see, Jerry was a year younger than I was. He was twelve and different from other people. He had entered this world as a Down's syndrome child. He looked different in a funny kind of way and had the mentality of a six-year-old. He also had a speech problem. His voice was low and gruff, and he'd often pronounce a lot of words wrong.

The difference had separated us, like seeds separate flowers. Yet we used to be close when we were young.

We laughed together, we cried together, and we stumbled through our younger years together. I had learned to understand Jerry and couldn't really see any difference between us.

But as the years came and went, I found other friends, and then came the realization of how different Jerry really was. This difference was an illness, a disease which took him from me and changed him continuously until he was no longer my brother. Instead, he became a simple animal in my eyes. He was an inhuman thing, which caused me enough embarrassment to make me hate him. I often became very cruel to him.

I remember on time when I had gone to play ball. As usual, Jerry would tag along with me. They wouldn't let me play because if a team let me play, they would have to take Jerry too, and nobody wanted him on their team. It had happened many times before, and each time, the resentment mounted.

One particular day was the end of the line for my patience, and I exploded at him. "Look, you stupid-looking creep. Why you gotta follow me around all the time? Leave me alone and go home." Then I slapped him again and again, and I wished he were dead. I just couldn't go anywhere without being embarrassed. Now my friends were referring to me as "the one with the MR for a brother." I didn't want to be embarrassed. Jerry finally went home crying.

I didn't really enjoy the game. I was too worried about the chewing out I'd be getting from Dad when I got home. To my surprise, but not really as I think back on it, when I got home, I discovered Jerry hadn't told on me. Instead, he met me at the door and apologized for making me mad.

I also remember one summer when we had gone to the beach. Naturally, I had to look out for Jerry. This was always my chore. All the kids started looking at us when they noticed Jerry was different. I couldn't take it and knew if I ignored him long enough he'd get lost. He did get lost, and he was gone for a long time. Everyone thought he'd drowned, and at the time, I couldn't have cared less. Hours later, an old man brought him back on top of his shoulders and said he'd found him about two miles down the beach behind an old outhouse, sitting in the sand and crying.

Well, time passed, leaves fell, and the snow came. Everyone looked forward to Christmas. I was looking at a dream of my own. There was this beautiful watch in the jeweler's window. A watch with a gold band. It really wasn't expensive but too expensive for us, for sure. I knew it was impossible, but I liked to imagine what it would be like wearing it on Christmas morning. Every time I passed the shop, I'd stand and stare at the watch.

I woke up Christmas morning, rushing to open the one gift wrapped for my by the fireplace. It was a great-looking sweater, and I really needed one too. "Thanks a lot, Dad!" I shouted. Then I noticed how tired Dad looked, so I asked him, "Did you stay up all night with Jerry again?"

"Yes," he replied. "Jerry's getting worse, I'm afraid."

You see about a week before, Jerry and I went tubing. Jerry ended up at the bottom of the hill, head down in a snowdrift. He lay there, kicking and squirming for help, but again, memories of past embarrassments brought out my cruelty, and I stood there and watched him for a minute before going to him. When I finally dug him out, instead of realizing what I had done, between his gasps for air and his tears, he tried to thank me for saving his life! Anyway, he'd caught pneumonia, and my parents had spent the last few nights up with him.

"Let's join your mother and Jerry," Dad said. Jerry's room smelt of medicine, and Jerry looked horrible lying there in his bed. His eyes were all lit up though, and he had a smile on his face. It looked to me like Mom had been crying. She sniffed softly and said, "Jerry's got a surprise for you, Jim."

I figured he was gonna hit me with another one of his awful butcher paper, water-colored type Christmas cards that he'd made. He tried to jump out of bed but soon found he was so weary he could barely move. He stumbled over to his closet and pulled another card out. Just what I thought. He got a flat sheet of poster paper about a square foot big and had written in water colors, "To my big brother, who I love the most."

As I glanced at the card, I noticed the broken pieces of his piggy bank in the corner. Then Jerry slowly reached under his bed and pulled out a small box. He wiped his nose with his PJ sleeve, stood there with his arms stretched out to me, and with all the love he could muster, said in his gruff voice, "Marwy Kwishmash, Shimay."

I opened the box and there, gleaming, reflecting the snowflakes through the window, lay the watch. The beautiful watch with the gold band, the watch I thought I'd never see again. I couldn't even stop looking at it.

Then Jerry gave me a big bear hug and asked, "Shimay, wars my pwesent?"

I looked up at him, then to the corner at the broken piggy bank, then to the shiny watch on my wrist, and then back to his questioning eyes. I didn't even have the courage to tell him that I'd forgotten about him. I just grabbed him and started bawling like a baby.

Jerry never lived to say "Happy New Year." He died two days later.

It's Christmas Eve and snowing again. I've just gotten off the phone. Mom and Dad had called to wish me a Merry Christmas. I lay back down on my dorm bed. I'm in college now. As I lay with my arms folded behind my head, I am looking at the only object on the wall—an old homemade, water-colored Christmas card. I look at my watch, the one with the gold band. Just a few seconds before midnight. It is almost Christmas.

I stare up at the wall again and read the words aloud, "To my big brother, who I love the most."

You know what? I could actually hear him say it again. "Marwy Kwishmash, Shimay." Only this time, I answered back. "Merry Christmas, Jerry. Merry Christmas."

—Gary Acevedo, Rise Leadership Group

AUTHOR'S INSIGHTS

Seeds that were planted: devotion, love, and forgiveness

Associated harvest: love, admiration, maturity, and respect

The yield is an understanding of the endless influence love will have in others lives as we freely give it away.

Love is often misunderstood. I don't speak of affection. I am talking about the love one person has for another. I'm talking about a kind of love that drives us to express gratitude, to be kind, to be patient, to share goodness, to show respect, and to try to make someone's life better. To believe and to hope that we can do something to ensure another person's happiness. To be like Jerry! This is a life with the greatest measure of yield.

YIELD IN ACTION NUMBER 8

GENEROSITY

The character trait of generosity claims our attention during the holiday season as well. The following story teaches us that quiet generosity can be found in the most unlikely places. As you read, I encourage you to think of the quiet ways you can make a difference in the lives of your family, colleagues, and customers.

The "Big Wheel"

In September 1960, I woke up one morning with six hungry babies and just seventy-five cents in my pocket. Their father was gone.

The boys ranged from three months to seven years, and their sister was two. If there was a welfare system in effect in southern Indiana at that time, I certainly knew nothing about it.

I scrubbed the kids until they looked brand-new and then put on my best homemade dress, loaded them into the rusty old 1951 Chevy, and drove off to find a job. The seven of us went to every factory, store, and restaurant in our small town.

No luck.

The kids stayed crammed into the car and tried to be quiet while I tried to convince whomever would listen that I was willing to learn or do anything. I had to have a job.

Still no luck.

The last place we went to, just a few miles out of town, was an old root beer barrel drive-in that had been converted into a truck stop. It was called the Big Wheel.

An older lady named Granny owned the place, and she peeked out of the window from time-to-time at all those kids.

She needed someone on the graveyard shift, eleven at night until seven in the morning. She paid sixty-five cents an hour, and I could start that night.

I raced home and called the teenager down the street that babysat for people. I bargained with her to come and sleep on my sofa for a dollar a night. She could arrive with her pajamas on, and the kids would already be asleep. This seemed like a good arrangement to her, so we made a deal.

That night, I started at the Big Wheel.

When I got home in the mornings, I woke the babysitter up and sent her home with one dollar of my tip money—fully half of what I averaged every night.

As the weeks went by, heating bills added a strain to my meager wage. The tires on the old Chevy had the consistency of penny balloons and began to leak. I had to fill them with air on the way to work and again every morning before I could go home.

One bleak fall morning after work, I dragged myself to the car to go home and found four tires in the back seat. New tires!

There was no note, no nothing, just those beautiful, brand-new tires. *Had angels taken up residence in Indiana?* I wondered.

I made a deal with the local service station. In exchange for mounting the tires, I would clean his office. I remember it took me a lot longer to scrub his floor than it did for him to install the tires.

I was now working six nights instead of five, and it still wasn't enough. Christmas was coming, and I knew there would be no money for toys for the kids.

I found a can of red paint and started repairing and painting some old toys. Then I hid them in the basement so there would be something for Santa to deliver on Christmas morning.

Clothes were a worry too. I was sewing patches on top of patches on the boys' pants, and soon, they would be too far gone to repair.

On Christmas Eve, the usual customers were drinking coffee in the Big Wheel. There were the truckers—Les, Frank, and Jim, and a state trooper named Joe. A few musicians were hanging around after a gig at the Legion and were dropping nickels in the pinball machine.

The regulars all just sat around and talked through the wee hours of the morning and then left to get home before the sun came up.

When it was time for me to go home at seven o'clock on Christmas morning, to my amazement, my old battered Chevy was filled full to the top with boxes of all shapes and sizes.

I quickly opened the driver's side door, crawled inside, and knelt in the front facing the backseat. Reaching back, I pulled off the lid of the top box. Inside was a whole case of little blue jeans, sizes 2–10!

I looked inside another box. It was full of shirts to go with the jeans.

Then I peeked inside some of the other boxes. There was candy and nuts and bananas and bags of groceries. There was an enormous ham for baking and canned vegetables and potatoes. There was pudding and Jell-O and cookies, pie filling, and flour. There was a whole bag of laundry supplies and cleaning items.

And there were five toy trucks and one beautiful little doll.

As I drove back through empty streets as the sun slowly rose on the most amazing Christmas Day of my life, I was sobbing with gratitude. And I will never forget the joy on the faces of my little ones that precious morning.

Yes, there were angels in Indiana that long-ago December. And they all hung out at the Big Wheel truck stop.

—Unknown Author Found on multiple websites including www.share-christmas.com

AUTHOR'S INSIGHTS

Seeds that were planted: compassion, generosity, caring, responsiveness, sincerity, and service

Associated harvest: gratitude, loyalty, friendship, and peace

The yield is an understanding that we are not alone in times of need. Conversely, we can lift another and be a source of strength and encouragement.

Living a life of yield includes a life of generosity and kindness. Oftentimes, your greatness is shown in an obscure location, like outside of town at the Big Wheel and when no one is even watching.

George W. Young said, "The greatness of a man or woman can nearly always be measured by their willingness to be kind."

You don't have to spend money to live a life of giving. Be generous with kind words and actions. Give a compliment to a family member, friend, colleague, customer, the wait staff at a restaurant, a cashier at the grocery store, or a complete stranger. It is guaranteed that a pleasant greeting or expression of appreciation can lift someone's day.

When possible, give of your resources, but giving of yourself can be the most generous act of kindness.

PS: It's also good for business. Generosity is a foundational component to the law of attraction.

YIELD IN ACTION NUMBER 9

HUMILITY

One Friday night in early October was the homecoming football game for the high school in our community. Shortly after the halftime events which included performances by the marching band, cheer leaders, and dance team, the homecoming royalty was announced.

During the introduction of the student royalty, I was reminded of the following story. It has been a number of years since I first read this story, and I still think it represents the greatest football event of all time—an event that continues to teach me of the need to have an educated heart. No matter what I do in life and in my career, the resounding lesson is to let my heart lead the way.

This story reveals that a depth of character can be developed at any age, and character is what can touch an entire community—and certainly your clients. It reinforces the golden rule of excellence in that "everything we do counts"—especially as we are involved in the great work of building character within ourselves.

Mature beyond their years, these five senior athletes made an ordinary homecoming football event extraordinary. They made a difference, and their example teaches that our ability to win in life can be measured by the size of our heart.

The Fixed Vote

It was halftime at the Lake Fenton–Mount Morris game, seemingly just another high school football contest during another homecoming week on a Friday night in another American suburb.

But this time, the fix was in motion.

Four Lake Fenton, Michigan, football players and a coconspirator on the golf team arranged it. Seniors all, they'd used their cell phones to hatch and agree on the plan and then met outside the school the afternoon before the big homecoming game to nail it down.

Lose on purpose?

Jake Kirk, the ringleader and a Blue Devils' running back, saw the decision differently. "We knew we'd all be winners if we did it."

By games end, they'd done it. The scoreboard at Lake Fenton Stadium unfortunately claimed the Blue Devils loss to Mount Morris 37–20, their lone defeat of the season so far.

But scoreboards can lie.

Last Friday, Kirk and fellow seniors David Bittinger, Lucas Hasenfratz, Matthew Tanneyhill and Ethan Merivirta scored one of the biggest victories of their lives.

Candidates for the senior royal crown, they each gave up the chance to become Lake Fenton's homecoming king.

They fixed it so Eli Florence won instead.

Eli is a 5' 7" former offensive lineman. He's only a sophomore. The doctors say there's nothing more they can do for him. He's at home, barely able to speak, getting regular blood transfusions. Eli Florence, fifteen, is dying of leukemia.

In these days filled, it seems, with it's-all-about-me athletes and iPod-wearing, text messaging teenagers, these Lake Fenton High athletes did something special for a special classmate.

"He's taught us never to give up," Kirk said. "And if you keep fighting, you can overcome the odds. We're happy he's still around because he wasn't supposed to be."

From one remission to two stem cell transplants to one stint of thirteen straight months in the hospital, from Flint to Ann Arbor to Minneapolis, and now back home, Eli Florence traveled and endured.

"Eli has become an icon for strength and perseverance and character for this entire community and especially our student body," said Lake Fenton principal, John Spicko.

But last month, the awful, final, numbing news came. Eli's mom wrote on a website set up by friends to monitor Eli's health, "Tonight I come with a broken heart. Eli has been given just a few weeks to live."

That was September 16. Word spread around the school and the town of about five thousand.

The nicest kid in school, the one who's out of class so often, was fading.

Then, it came to Jake Kirk, as crisply and clearly as his two syllable name: Eli should be homecoming king.

Kirk phoned Tanneyhill. Tanneyhill was with Hasenfratz. Before Kirk even got the entire concept out of his mouth, "They immediately said yes," Kirk said. Soon after, the other two senior candidates for homecoming readily agreed as well.

By lunchtime, they'd planned their announcement for what was to be the king candidate-selection assembly.

Kirk took the microphone in front of the entire student body of 538 students and said there wouldn't be any vote for king this year.

"We, as the king's court, decided that nobody deserves this more than Eli Florence. This year's homecoming king is going to be Eli."

The entire audience cheered and clapped in unison.

But Eli was too sick to be in school that day.

"The whole school knew, but Eli did not know," Sticko said.

That night, Eli's mom received a text message telling her that Eli would be crowned the next night at halftime of the football game. She didn't tell her son.

Halftime was approaching, and the king-to-be was at a local clinic, receiving a necessary blood transfusion, getting energy, getting life. He was scheduled to escort his friend, Ashley Look, a member of the sophomore royal court, to midfield. He didn't have a clue he would be the center of attention.

Barely in the nick of time, Eli, in a wheelchair, and Ashley joined the other members of the court and their parents at midfield, surrounded by the Lake Fenton band, clad in blue and white.

The public address announcer said, "Your 2007 king, as designated by the five candidates is…is Eli Florence."

The king was stunned.

"But I'm not a senior," Eli told others around him. "I'm not a senior."

The crowd of two thousand people, including homecoming queen Brooke Hull, seventeen, stood, and many cried.

That night, the winners were not decided by the numbers on the scoreboard. They were winners before the game even started.

—Condensed from a report by
Jay Weiner, ESPN.com

AUTHOR'S INSIGHTS

Seeds that were planted: generosity, compassion, respect, leadership, and humility

Associated harvest: gratitude, honor, value, and belief

The yield is learning what matters most and realizing that the greatest victories in life are not able to be measured by the final numbers on a scoreboard.

I hope you'll think of this football event from time to time throughout your life and career. It is sometimes only through your heart that you can see correctly.

When you lead with your heart, you will always win. Your character shines through, and this will prove to be your greatest asset. If you are helping a friend, meeting with a client, performing an evaluation with an employee, meeting with a colleague, or in general conversation throughout the organization, you can make a difference. Lead with your heart, and you will experience an increased yield in your life.

> What you get by achieving your goals is not as important as what you become by achieving your goals.
>
> —Zig Ziglar

YIELD IN ACTION NUMBER 10

APPRECIATION

The following story provides some profound insights on how to be successful in business and in life.

The Portrait

A wealthy man and his son loved to collect rare works of art. They had everything in their collection from Picasso to Raphael. They often sat together and admired these great works of art.

When the Vietnam conflict broke out, the son went to war. He was very courageous and died in battle while rescuing another soldier. The father was notified and grieved deeply for his only son.

About a month later, there was a knock at the door. A young man stood at the door with a large package in his hands.

He said, "Sir, you don't know me, but I am the soldier for whom your son gave his life. He saved many lives that day, and he was carrying me to safety when a bullet struck him, and he died instantly. He often talked about you and your love for art." The young man held out a package. "I know this isn't much. I'm not really a great artist, but I think your son would have wanted you to have this."

The father opened the package. It was a portrait of his son painted by the young man. He stared in awe at the way the soldier had captured the personality of his son in the painting. The father was so drawn to the eyes that his own eyes welled up with tears. He thanked the young man and offered to pay him for the picture. "Oh no, sir. I could never repay what your son did for me. It's a gift."

The father hung the portrait over his mantle. Every time visitors came to his home, he took them to see the portrait of his son before he showed them any of the other great works he had collected.

The man died a few years later. There was to be a great auction of his paintings. Many influential people gathered, excited over seeing the great paintings and having an opportunity to purchase one for their collection.

On the platform sat the painting of the son. The auctioneer pounded his gavel. "We will start the bidding with this picture of the son. Who will bid for this picture?"

There was silence.

Then a voice in the back of the room shouted, "We want to see the famous paintings. Skip this one."

But the auctioneer persisted. "Will somebody bid for this painting? Who will start the bidding? $100, $200?"

Another voice angrily said, "We didn't come to see this painting. We came to see the Van Goghs, the Rembrandts. Get with the real bids!"

But still the auctioneer continued, "The son! The son! Who'll take the son?"

Finally, a voice came from the very back of the room. It was the longtime gardener of the man and his son. "I'll give $10 for the painting." Being a poor man, it was all he could afford.

"We have $10. Who will bid $20?"

"Give it to him for $10. Let's see the masters."

"Ten dollars is bid. Won't someone bid $20?" said the auctioneer.

The crowd was becoming angry. They didn't want the picture of his son. They wanted the more worthy investments for the collections.

The auctioneer pounded the gavel. "Going once, twice… Sold for $10."

A man sitting on the second row shouted, "Now let's get on with the collection!"

The auctioneer laid down his gavel. "I'm sorry. The auction is over."

"What about the paintings?"

"I am sorry. When I was called to conduct this auction, I was told of a secret stipulation in the will. I was not allowed to reveal that stipulation until this time. Only the painting of the son would be auctioned. Whoever bought that painting would inherit the entire estate, including all the paintings. The man in the back who took the son gets everything!"

—Unknown Author Found on multiple websites including www.snopes.com

AUTHOR'S INSIGHTS

Seeds that were planted: honor, respect, appreciation, and sensitivity

Associated harvest: affection, prosperity, loyalty, and value

The yield was a realization that your success will come in the way you treat others and respect what is important to them.

One lesson to be learned from this story is that you need to recognize and respect what others deem to be valuable. When you are respectful to your customers, colleagues, family, friends, an employee at a store, or anyone who simply crosses your path, they will almost always return to you that same respect in kind.

Knowing how to show respect for others may be one of the most significant character traits you can develop in living a life with yield in mind. It will be influential in your business success as well as in every area of your life.

It is equally important to glean from this story the importance of completing a thorough self-evaluation from time to time. You may not realize how you come across to others without taking a step back and taking a look at yourself. Are you impatient—wanting only to get to the works of art that are important to you? Are you demanding—pushing things along at a rate that meets your schedule?

Similarly, throughout every position within your organization, you need to consistently take a look at yourself from your customer's point of view. Evaluate your company culture, your attitudes, your strengths, and your weaknesses. Then, consider how these things are influencing your success, and take the necessary steps to make improvements where needed. Use the Change Order when needed.

In general, what characteristics do you want your portrait to portray? Does your current direction capture your personality?

An anonymous author wrote, "Our background and circumstances may have influenced who we are, but we are responsible for who we become."

One last idea for those readers who are of the Christian faith: a third lesson from this story is simply a reminder that when you take the Son, you get everything!

YIELD IN ACTION NUMBER 11

INSPIRATION

This message will take you back in time to memories of your first telephone (at least for those of us born by the 1960s). There are many lessons to be learned about life, business, and success through this story. As you will see, even through brief encounters with those around you, you can make a meaningful impression on others. Don't underestimate your incredible value and the small ways you can increase your yield.

Information Please

When I was quite young, my father had one of the first telephones in our neighborhood. I remember well the polished old case fastened to the wall. The shiny receiver hung on the side of the box. I was too little to reach the telephone but used to listen with fascination when my mother used to talk to it. Then I discovered that somewhere inside the wonderful device lived an amazing person—her name was Information Please, and there was nothing she did not know.

Information Please could supply anybody's number and the correct time.

My first personal experience with this genie in the bottle came one day while my mother was visiting a neighbor. Amusing myself at the tool bench in the basement, I whacked my finger with a hammer. The pain was terrible, but there didn't seem to be any reason for crying because there was no one home to give sympathy. I walked around the house sucking my throbbing finger, finally arriving at the stairway. *The telephone*, I thought.

Quickly, I ran for the footstool in the parlor and dragged it to the landing. Climbing up, I unhooked the receiver in the parlor and held it to my ear. "Information Please," I said into the mouthpiece just above my head. A click or two and a small clear voice spoke into my ear.

"Information."

"I hurt my finger," I wailed into the phone. The tears came readily enough now that I had an audience.

"Isn't your mother home?" came the question.

"Nobody's home but me," I blubbered.

"Are you bleeding?"

"No," I replied. "I hit my finger with the hammer, and it hurts."

"Can you open your icebox?" she asked. I said I could.

"Then chip off a little piece of ice and hold it to your finger," said the voice.

After that, I called Information Please for everything. I asked her for help with my geography, and she told me where Philadelphia was. She helped me with my math. She even told me my pet chipmunk that I had caught in the park just the day before would eat fruits and nuts.

Then, there was the time Petey, our pet canary, died. I called Information Please and told her the sad story. She listened, then said the usual things grownups say to soothe a child. But I was unconsoled. I asked her, "Why is it that birds should sing so beautifully and bring joy to all families, only to end up as a heap of feathers on the bottom of a cage?" She must have sensed my deep concern, for she said quietly, "Paul, always remember that there are other worlds to sing in."

Somehow I felt better.

Another day I was on the telephone. "Information Please."

"Information," said the now familiar voice.

"How do you spell fix?" I asked.

All this took place in a small town in the Pacific Northwest.

When I was nine years old, we moved across the country to Boston. I missed my friend very much. Information Please belonged in that old wooden box back home, and I somehow never thought of trying the tall, shiny new phone that sat on the table in the hall.

As I grew into my teens, the memories of those childhood conversations never really left me. Often, in moments of doubt and perplexity, I would recall the serene sense of security I had then. I appreciated now how patient, understanding, and kind she was to have spent her time on a little boy.

A few years later, on my way west to college, my plane put down in Seattle. I had about half an hour or so between planes. I spent fifteen minutes or so on the phone with my sister who lived there now.

Then without thinking what I was doing, I dialed my hometown operator and said, "Information, please."

Miraculously, I heard the small, clear voice I knew so well. "Information."

I hadn't planned this, but I heard myself saying, "Could you please tell me how to spell fix?"

There was a long pause then came the soft-spoken answer, "I guess your finger must have healed by now."

"So it's really still you," I said. "I wonder if you have any idea how much you meant to me during that time."

"I wonder," she said, "if you know how much your calls meant to me. I never had any children, and I used to look forward to your calls."

I told her how often I had thought of her over the years, and I asked if I could call her again when I came back to visit my sister.

"Please do," she said. "Just ask for Sally."

Three months later, I was back in Seattle. A different voice answered, "Information." I asked for Sally.

"Are you a friend?" she said.

"Yes, a very old friend," I answered.

She paused. "I'm sorry to have to tell you this," she said. "Sally had been working part-time the last few years because she was sick. She died five weeks ago."

I was stunned. Before I could hang up, she said, "Wait a minute. Did you say your name was Paul?"

"Yes."

"Well, Sally left a message for you. She wrote it down in case you called. Let me read it to you." The note says, 'Tell him I still say there are other worlds to sing in. He'll know what I mean.'"

I thanked her and hung up. I knew what Sally meant.

—Paul Villard as presented in the June 1966
Reader's Digest

AUTHOR'S INSIGHTS

Seeds that were planted: learning, service, courage, understanding, and encouragement

Associated harvest: wisdom, admiration, love, appreciation, and friendship

The yield was a greater appreciation of inspiration and an understanding that wisdom comes with experience as well as the responsibility to share it with others.

Never underestimate the positive impression you can make on others. This applies to everyone you come in contact with—your family, friends, children, spouse, customers, and colleagues. Many will look to you for information, compassion, encouragement, and reassurance.

In terms of your business success, you can help build a client's confidence in you and their own self-worth simply by the attention you give to them and the information you provide.

Planting the seeds that will allow you to harvest someone's confidence in you will prove to be a distinct competitive advantage in your business success and lead to a greater yield.

Make sure you are available for your spouse, children, colleagues, and customers. Spend time developing a relationship with them. Provide meaningful, relevant, and accurate information. Become involved in their needs as if they were your own. Sally mastered this skill and was there when it mattered most. The good news is that this is not hard; it's a matter of the heart, and you can do it.

Don't underestimate the value of providing loving Information—Please!

YIELD IN ACTION NUMBER 12

EXAMPLE AND FINDING A BIGGER PURPOSE

As customers would come through the door of my company and I had the opportunity to spend time with them, I was always hopeful that I was giving them the best advice possible. Sometimes that meant that I had to tell them that I was not their best solution.

Helping others is the right thing to do. I believe the following story helps demonstrate what I mean.

Three Red Marbles

I was at the corner grocery store, buying some early potatoes. I noticed a small boy, delicate of bone and feature, ragged but clean, hungrily appraising a basket of freshly picked green peas.

I paid for my potatoes but was also drawn to the display of fresh green peas. I am a pushover for creamed peas and new potatoes.

Pondering the peas, I couldn't help overhearing the conversation between Mr. Miller (the store owner) and the ragged boy next to me.

"Hello, Barry, how are you today?"

"H'lo, Mr. Miller. Fine, thank ya. Jus' admirin' them peas. They sure look good."

"They are good, Barry. How's your ma?"

"Fine. Gittin' stronger alla' time."

"Good. Anything I can help you with?"

"No, sir. Jus' admirin' them peas."

"Would you like to take some home?" asked Mr. Miller.

"No, sir. Got nuthin' to pay for 'em with."

"Well, what have you to trade me for some of those peas?"

"All I got's my prize marble here."

"Is that right? Let me see it," said Miller.

"Here 'tis. She's a dandy."

"I can see that. Hmm, only thing is this one is blue, and I sort of go for red. Do you have a red one like this at home?" the store owner asked.

"Not zackley, but almost…"

"Tell you what. Take this sack of peas home with you, and next trip this way, let me look at that red marble," Mr. Miller told the boy.

"Sure will. Thanks, Mr. Miller."

Mrs. Miller, who had been standing nearby, came over to help me. With a smile, she said, "There are two other boys like him in our community, all three are in very poor circumstances. Jim just loves to bargain with them for peas, apples, tomatoes, or whatever. When they come back with their red marbles, and they always do, he decides he doesn't like red after all, and he sends them home with a bag of produce for a green marble or an orange one when they come on their next trip to the store."

I left the store smiling to myself, impressed with this man. A short time later, I moved to Colorado, but I never forgot the story of this man, the boys, and their bartering for marbles.

Several years went by, each more rapid than the previous one. Just recently, I had occasion to visit some old friends in that Idaho community, and while I was there, I learned that Mr. Miller had died.

They were having his visitation that evening, and knowing my friends wanted to go, I agreed to accompany them. Upon arrival at the mortuary, we got in line to meet the relatives of the deceased and to offer whatever words of comfort we could.

Ahead of us in line were three young men. One was in an army uniform and the other two wore nice haircuts, dark suits, and white shirts—all very professional looking. They approached Mrs. Miller, who was standing composed and smiling by her husband's casket. Each of the young men hugged her, kissed her on the cheek, spoke briefly with her, and moved on to the casket.

Her misty light blue eyes followed them as, one by one, each young man stopped and briefly placed his hand over her husbands. Each left the mortuary awkwardly, wiping his eyes.

Our turn came to meet Mrs. Miller. I told her who I was and reminded her of the story from those many years ago and what she had told me about her husband's bartering for marbles. With her eyes glistening, she took my hand and led me to the casket.

"Those three young men who just left were the boys I told you about. They just told me how they appreciated the things Jim 'traded' them. Now, at last, when Jim could not change his mind about color or size, they came to pay their debt."

"We've never had a great deal of the wealth of this world," she confided. "But right now, Jim would consider himself the richest man in Idaho."

With loving gentleness, she lifted the lifeless fingers of her husband. Resting underneath were three exquisitely shined red marbles.

—William E. Petersen as presented in the
1975 October *Ensign* Magazine

AUTHOR'S INSIGHTS

Seeds that were planted: compassion, understanding, caring, and responsiveness

Associated harvest: love, respect, appreciation, friendship, and promotion

The yield was learning that living an exemplary and purpose-driven life will far outweigh any value that may be accumulated in our bank accounts.

Helping others with no expected return marks one of the highest levels of selfless service we can offer. Always remember: "it's not what you gather but what you scatter that tells what kind of life you have lived."

YIELD IN ACTION NUMBER 13

TIME

When I was becoming a proficient coloring book artist in elementary school, the simple advice was to "stay inside the lines." My choice of colors and artistic flair seemed less important than my accuracy. I just remember being complimented when I exerted enough hand control to not go outside the lines.

Last year while driving home after a long day, I was pulled over by a state patrolman. It seems that I was not paying close enough attention, and I had crossed the center line a couple of times which caused him to question if I had been drinking? After a short conversation, it was obvious that I was just a poor driver. His advice: "Keep Inside the Lines."

In life and business, there is a lesson to be learned about keeping inside the lines. It is easy to get so busy doing good things that we can miss an opportunity to do something truly great with our time. We must be alert and aware of how we can positively influence each moment. Don't let yourself be distracted from realizing what can be the best use of your time simply because you are engaged in good activities.

Mac Anderson and Lance Wubbels provide the following story that helps bring this to into clarity.

The Journal

In the faint light of an attic, an old man, tall and stooped, made his way to a stack of boxes near a half window. Brushing aside a wisp of cobwebs, he tilted the top box toward the light and began to carefully lift out one old photograph album after another.

His search began with the fond recollection of the love of his life, long gone. Somewhere in these albums was a photo of her he hoped to rediscover. Patiently opening the long buried treasures, he soon was lost in a sea of memories. Although his world had not stopped spinning when his wife left it, the past was more alive in his heart than his present loneliness.

Setting beside one of the dusty albums, he pulled from the box what appeared to be a journal from his grown son's childhood. He could not recall ever having seen it before or that his son had ever kept a journal. Opening the yellowed pages, he glanced over a short reading, and his lips curved in an unconscious smile. Even his eyes brightened as he read the words that spoke clear and sweet to his soul. It was the voice of a little boy that had grown up far to fast in his very house.

In the utter silence of the attic, the words of a guileless six-year-old worked their magic and carried the old man back to a time almost totally forgotten. Entry after entry stirred a sentimental hunger in his heart, but it was accompanied by the painful memory that his son's simple recollections of those days were far different from his own.

But how different? Reminded that he had kept a daily journal of his business activities over the years, he closed his son's journal and turned to leave, having forgotten the cherished photo that had triggered his search. Hunched over to keep from bumping his head on the rafters, the old man stepped to the wooden stairway and made his descent to the den.

Opening a glass cabinet door, he reached in and pulled out an old business journal, then placed the two journals beside each other. His was leather-bound, engraved with his name in gold, while his son's was tattered and the name Jimmy had been nearly scuffed from its surface.

He ran a long skinny finger over the letters, as though he could restore what had been worn away with time and use. As he opened his journal, his eyes fell upon an inscription that stood out because it was so brief in comparison to other days. In his own neat handwriting were these words: "Wasted the whole day with Jimmy. Didn't catch a thing."

With a deep sigh and a shaking hand, he took Jimmy's journal and found the boy's entry for the same day, June 4. Large scrawling letters pressed deeply into the paper read, "Went fishing with my dad today. Best day of my life."

Remember: to the world you may just be one person, but to one person, you might just be the world.

THE LAW OF THE YIELD

AUTHOR'S INSIGHTS

Seeds that were planted: respect, time, reflection, and courage

Associated harvest: love, appreciation, tenderness, and value

The yield was an understanding of the importance of taking time to do the little things. Our value is defined by the small things we do every day.

In building your life of yield, remember that love is spelled T-I-M-E. Make sure you keep the demands on your time in balance. Yes, devote the necessary attention to be successful in your business pursuits, but don't allow them to compromise the most rewarding moments of your life.

In the poem "The Dash," the author describes a funeral in which the speaker identified his friend's date of birth and date of death but said that what really mattered was the dash between those dates. One line in particular reads, "So as you conclude your life, the question becomes clear, will you be proud of the dash that has defined your years?"

Carefully consider the best use of your time. Your choices ultimately define your dash and your yield.

YIELD IN ACTION NUMBER 14

HEART

Your personal touch is far more powerful and lasting in someone's life than you may realize. Your family and those around you are especially influenced by your time and personal attention. As you will find in the following story, you can make a difference in the outcome of an event when you take the time to lead with your heart.

A $1.11 Miracle

A little girl named Tess went to her bedroom and pulled a glass jelly jar from its hiding place in the closet.

She poured the change out on the floor and counted it carefully. Three times even. The total had to be exactly perfect. No chance here for mistakes.

Carefully placing the coins back in the jar and twisting on the cap, she slipped out the back door and made her way six blocks to Rexall's Drug Store.

She waited patiently for the pharmacist to give her some attention, but he was too busy at this moment.

Tess twisted her feet to make a scuffing noise. Nothing. She cleared her throat with the most disgusting sound she could muster. No good.

Finally, she took a quarter from her jar and banged it on the glass counter. That did the trick!

"And what can I do for you?" the pharmacist asked in an annoyed tone of voice. "I'm talking to my brother from Chicago whom I haven't seen in ages," he said without waiting for a reply to his question.

"Well, I want to talk to you about my brother," Tess answered. "He's really, really sick...and I want to buy a miracle."

"I beg your pardon?" said the pharmacist.

"His name is Andrew, and he has something bad growing inside his head, and my daddy says only a miracle can save him now. So how much does a miracle cost?"

"We don't sell miracles here, little girl. I'm sorry but I can't help you," the pharmacist said.

"Listen, I have the money to pay for it. If it isn't enough, I will get the rest. Just tell me how much it costs."

The pharmacist's brother was a well-dressed man. He stooped down and asked the little girl, "What kind of a miracle does your brother need?"

"I don't know," Tess replied with her eyes welling up with tears. "I just know he's really sick, and Mommy says he needs an operation. But Daddy said they can't pay for it, so I want to use my money."

"How much do you have?" asked the man from Chicago.

"One dollar and eleven cents," Tess answered barely audibly. "It's all the money I have, but I can get some more if I need to."

"Well, what a coincidence," said the man and smiled. "A dollar and eleven cents—the exact price of a miracle for little brothers."

He took her money in one hand, and with the other hand, he grasped her mitten and said, "Take me to where you live. I want to see your brother and meet your parents. Let's see if I have the miracle you need."

That well-dressed man was Dr. Carlton Armstrong, a surgeon, specializing in neurosurgery.

After evaluating Andrew's condition, he made all the arrangements. The operation was completed, free of charge, and it wasn't long until Andrew was home again and doing well.

Mom and Dad were happily talking about the chain of events that had led them to this place. "That surgery," her mom whispered, "was a real miracle. I wonder how much it would have cost?"

Tess smiled. She knew exactly how much a miracle cost. "One dollar and eleven cents."

—Unknown Author Found on multiple websites including www.moral-stories.org

AUTHOR'S INSIGHTS

Seeds that were planted: love, generosity, potential, hope, faith, humility, and pptimism

Associated harvest: miracle, gratitude, wisdom, respect, and appreciation

The yield was a realization that we can have a positive influence in others lives through our faith and service to them. Belief and optimism win over hopelessness and doubt.

Miracles can happen in our lives when we are aware of other's needs. It's the small things that can make the biggest difference in your yield—a phone call, a handshake, a short handwritten note giving recognition for a job well done, lending a listening ear, or just offering a word of encouragement.

Don't underestimate the power of your personal touch and involvement. It is the one thing that will linger the longest in another person's life.

The following poem was recited in an interview with the great UCLA basketball coach, John Wooden. He was talking about how he felt his role as a coach was really that of a teacher. I believe it can apply to most any profession, but certainly, it applies to us personally. He said we are all teachers by the way we live our life and the way we influence those around us through our example. He recited,

> No written word,
> Nor spoken plea;
> Can teach our youth
> What they should be.
> Nor all the books
> On all the shelves;
> It's what the teachers
> Are themselves.

Please know that there are many around you watching, learning, and following your positive example.

YIELD IN ACTION NUMBER 15

RESPECT

It is inspiring when we see someone showing greatness of character. It helps us become aware of our own potential to make a difference in someone else's life. An example of greatness may be seen in a small third-grade classroom, it may be seen in front of thousands of people, or it may be through the evidence left behind from an anonymous donor.

A wonderful example of greatness of character and generosity is shown in a softball game that made national news in 2009, and it wasn't because of the final score.

A Home Run for Sara

With two runners on base and a strike against her, Sara Tucholsky of Western Oregon University uncorked her best swing and did something she had never done in high school or college. Her first home run ever cleared the centerfield fence.

But it appeared to be the shortest of dreams come true when, in her excitement, she missed first base and upon her return to the bag, she tore a ligament in her knee and collapsed.

She crawled back to first base but could not continue around the bases. The first-base coach said she would be called out if her teammates tried to help her, and the umpire said a pinch runner could be called in, but the home run would only count as a single.

Central Washington's first baseman, Mallory Holtman, who was the career home run leader in the Great Northwest Athletic Conference, asked the umpire if she and her teammates could help Tucholsky?

The umpire said there was no rule against it.

Then, members of the Central Washington University softball team stunned spectators by carrying Tucholsky around the bases so the tree-run home run would count—an act that contributed to their own elimination from the playoffs.

Holtman and shortstop, Liz Wallace, put their arms under Tucholsky's legs as she put her arms over their shoulders. The three headed around the base path, stopping to let Tucholsky touch each base with her good leg.

"The only thing I remember is that Mallory asked me which leg was the one that hurt," Tucholsky said. "I told her it was my right leg, and she said, 'Okay, we're going to drop you down gently, and you need to touch it with your left leg,' and I said, 'Okay, thank you very much.'"

She said, "You deserve it. You hit it over the fence."

"We didn't know she was a senior nor that this was her first home run," Wallace said. "That makes the story more touching than it was at the time. We just wanted to help her."

Holtman said she and Wallace weren't thinking about the playoff spot and didn't consider the gesture as something others wouldn't do.

"I hope I would do the same for her in the same situation," Tucholsky added.

As the trio reached home plate, the entire Western Oregon team was in tears.

Central Washington coach Gary Frederick, a fourteen-year coaching veteran, called the act of sportsmanship "unbelievable."

Tucholsky's injury will sideline her for the rest of the season. Her home run sent Western Oregon to a 4–2 victory, ending Central Washington's chances of winning the conference and advancing to the playoffs.

"In the end, it is not about winning and losing so much," Holtman said. "It was about this girl. She hit it over the fence and was in pain, and she deserved a home run."

—FOXSports.com, NBCSports.com and many others similarly reported the details of this story

AUTHOR'S INSIGHTS

Seeds that were planted: generosity, compassion, respect, leadership, and humility

Associated harvest: gratitude, honor, value, admiration, and nobility

The yield was a realization that doing the right thing is always the right thing to do.

Think of what you can do today to carry someone's load or, at least, make it a little lighter. What could you do for a member of your family, a friend, or a complete stranger who is feeling the weight of the world on their shoulders?

Do the unexpected by looking for ways to be generous and helpful. Unsolicited help is more appreciated than when it is requested. It takes an educated heart, but you have one. Listen and it will lead you in the right direction.

Collaborate personally with your family and friends and professionally with your colleagues as you search for ways to help others. The weight you can collectively carry is far greater, and the burden lightened when you work together. That is what makes this life so wonderful. You are never carrying the entire weight of your dreams by yourself!

YIELD IN ACTION NUMBER 16

GOODNESS

We make a variety of choices every day. While most may seem small, others can change your life and the life of those around you. It is important to realize the influence your choices have on others. What we do or don't do matters.

We learn a valuable lesson from the following group of young boys and the choices they made while playing a baseball game.

Can I Play

Shay and his father were walking past a park where some boys Shay knew were playing baseball. Shay asked, "Do you think they'll let me play?" Shay's father knew that most of the boys would not want someone like Shay on their team, but his father also understood that if his son were allowed to play, it would give him a much-needed sense of belonging and joy to be accepted by others in spite of his handicaps.

Shay's father approached one of the boys on the field and asked if Shay could play, not expecting much. The boy looked around for guidance and said, "We're losing by six runs, and the game is in the eighth inning. I guess he can be on our team, and we'll try to let him play in the ninth inning."

Shay struggled over to the team's bench, put on a team shirt with a broad smile, and his father had a small tear in his eye and warmth in his heart. The boys saw the father's joy at his son being accepted. In the bottom of the eighth inning, Shay's team scored a few runs but was still behind by three. In the top of the ninth inning, Shay put on a glove and played in right field. Even though no hits came his way, he was obviously ecstatic just to be in the game and on the field, grinning from ear to ear as his father waved to him from the stands.

In the bottom of the ninth inning, Shay's team scored again. Now, with two outs and the bases loaded, the potential winning run was on base, and Shay was scheduled to be next at bat.

At this juncture, do they let Shay bat and give away their chance to win the game? Surprisingly, Shay was given a bat. Everyone knew that a hit was all but impossible because Shay didn't really know how to hold the bat properly, much less connect with the ball.

However, as Shay stepped up to the plate, the pitcher, recognizing the other team had put winning aside, moved in a few steps to lob the ball softly so Shay could at least make contact. The first pitch came, and Shay swung clumsily and missed. The pitcher again took a few steps forward to toss the ball even more softly toward Shay. As the pitch came in, Shay swung at the ball and hit a slow ground ball right back to the pitcher.

The pitcher picked up the soft grounder and could have easily thrown the ball to the first baseman. Shay would have been out and that would have been the end of the game. Instead, the pitcher threw the ball right over the head of the first baseman, out of reach of all his teammates. Everyone from the stands and both teams started yelling, "Shay, run to first! Run to first!"

Never in his life had Shay ever ran that far, but he made it to first base. He scampered down the baseline, wide-eyed and startled.

Everyone yelled, "Run to second! Run to second!"

Catching his breath, Shay awkwardly ran toward second, gleaming and struggling to make it to second base. By the time Shay rounded toward second base, the right fielder had the ball, the smallest guy on their team, who had a chance to be the hero for his team for the first time. He could have thrown the ball to the second baseman for the tag, but he understood the pitcher's intentions, and he too intentionally threw the ball high and far over the third baseman's head.

Shay ran toward third base, as everyone shouted, "Run to third! Shay, run to third!" As Shay rounded third, the boys from both teams and those watching were on their feet and screaming, "Shay, run home!" Shay ran to home, stepped on the plate, and was cheered as the hero who hit the "grand slam" and won the game for his team.

That day the boys from both teams helped bring a piece of true love and humanity into the world.

Shay didn't make it to another summer and died that winter. He never forgot being the hero and making his father so happy and coming home to have his mother tearfully embrace her little hero of the day!

—Unknown Author Found on multiple websites including www.just4kidsmagazine.com

AUTHOR'S INSIGHTS

Seeds that were planted: understanding, sacrifice, generosity, compassion, virtue, and leadership

Associated harvest: goodness, honor, integrity, self-respect, and cooperation

The yield was an understanding that goodness spreads—that you can lead others to make great decisions through your example. Your realm of influence is far greater than you can possibly imagine.

What a magical moment! It was magical not only for Shay and his dad and mom, but for all those watching and for each young boy that participated. Goodness is a key to living a life of meaningful yield.

When sensitivity to others is in the forefront of our thoughts, we will become the creator of magical moments as well. Think of how things could be if we all tried to remain aware of others while we are going about our own daily tasks. I believe we would see acts of love and humanity filling the world.

These boys understood the lessons they had been taught and were able to apply it in their lives at a time when it mattered most. They realized that winning is not measured by the final score but by the final choices they make.

Therefore, I encourage you to think of what you can do for a family member, friend, colleague, or complete stranger. I promise that some of the most rewarding experiences in your life will be when you are doing something for someone else.

> Do not let what you cannot do interfere with what you can do.
>
> —John Wooden

YIELD IN ACTION NUMBER 17

SUCCESS

It is easy for us to focus on our own needs and the things that matter most to us. In the course of our day, we can easily overlook what we can do for others. However, *love* is the great equalizer. It allows, or might I even say, it requires us to focus our attention on others first.

We have *today* and there is always *tomorrow*, but it is most important that we realize what we can do *now*. Now is the time we can make a difference. Now

GREG MCCLANAHAN

is the time that we have the most control over. Now is the time to choose the best use of our energy. Now will further define who we are. And the best way to determine what to do next is to listen to our heart.

The following story beautifully exemplifies this idea.

Puppies for Sale

A farmer had some puppies that were ready to sell. He painted a sign advertising the four pups and set about to nail the sign to a post on the edge of his yard. As he was driving the last nail into the post, he felt a tug on his overalls. He looked down into the eyes of a little boy.

"Mister," he said, "I want to buy one of your puppies."

"Well," said the farmer as he rubbed the sweat off the back of his neck, "these puppies come from fine parents and cost a good deal of money."

The boy dropped his head for a moment. Then reaching deep into his pocket, he pulled out a handful of change and held it up to the farmer.

"I've got thirty-nine cents. Is that enough to take a look?"

"Sure," said the farmer. And with that, he let out a whistle. "Here, Dolly!" he called. Out from the doghouse and down the ramp ran Dolly and was followed by four little balls of fur.

The little boy pressed his face against the chain-link fence. His eyes danced with delight. A smile lit up his entire face.

As the dogs made their way to the fence, the little boy noticed something else stirring inside the doghouse. Slowly, another little ball appeared. This one

162

was noticeably smaller. Down the ramp, it slid. Then in a somewhat awkward manner, the little pup began hobbling toward the others, doing its best to catch up.

"I want that one," the little boy said, pointing to the runt. The farmer knelt down at the boy's side and said, "Son, you don't want that puppy. He will never be able to run and play with you like these other dogs would."

With that, the little boy stepped back from the fence, reached down, and began rolling up one leg of his trousers.

In doing so, he revealed a steel brace running down both sides of his leg attaching itself to a specially made shoe.

Looking back up at the farmer, he said, "You see, sir, I don't run too well myself, and he will need someone who understands."

With tears in his eyes, the farmer reached down and picked up the little pup.

Holding it carefully, he handed it to the little boy.

"How much do I owe you?" asked the little boy.

"No charge," answered the farmer. "There's no charge for love."

—Unknown Author Found on multiple websites including www.spiritual-short-stories.com

AUTHOR'S INSIGHTS

Seeds that were planted: charity, generosity, compassion, love, and virtue

Associated harvest: value, courage, empathy, and gratitude

The yield was learning that when love directs our actions, we can achieve a greater result. It is through an educated heart that we can consistently achieve greater outcomes.

Love and understanding are foundational to our success. For some, too much of life can be about what they are able to get. The farmer in this story understood what Winston Churchill said when he stated, "We make a living by what we get. We make a life by what we give."

The challenge today and each day is to choose the best way to spend each moment. Take time to stop and help someone along the way through life. Remember that the most important things in life are not things and that yield is often not measurable by a scale.

YIELD IN ACTION NUMBER 18

COURAGE

It is important to try to always remember your own value as well as the value of those around you. In many ways, you have made sacrifices throughout your lifetime for your family, your children, your grandchildren, and quite possibly, your country. The following stories tell how a love for others and the knowledge of a person's value drove two men to make remarkable sacrifices.

A Successful Mission

During the course of World War II, many people gained fame in one way or another. One man was Butch O'Hare. He was a fighter pilot assigned to an aircraft carrier in the Pacific. One time, his entire squadron was assigned to fly a particular mission. After he was airborne, he looked at his fuel gauge and realized that someone had forgotten to top off his fuel tank. Because of this, he would not have enough fuel to complete his flight and get back to his ship. So his leader told him to leave formation and return.

As he was returning to the mother ship, he could see a squadron of Japanese Zeroes heading toward the fleet to attack. With all the fighter planes gone, the fleet was almost defenseless.

His was the only opportunity to distract and divert them. Single handedly, he dove into the Japanese planes and attacked them.

The American fighter planes were rigged with cameras, so that as they flew and fought, pictures were taken so they were able to learn more about the terrain, enemy planes, etc.

Butch dove at them and shot until all his ammunition was gone; then, he would dive and try to clip off a wing or tail or anything that would make them unfit to fly. He did anything he could to keep them from reaching the American ships.

Finally, the Japanese squadron took off in another direction. Butch O'Hare and his fighter, both badly shot-up, limped back to the carrier.

He told his story, but not until the film from the camera on his plane was developed did they realize the extent he really went to, to protect his fleet.

He was recognized as a hero and given one of the highest honors. And as you know, the O'Hare Airport was also named after him.

Easy Eddie

There was a man named Easy Eddie who lived in Chicago. He was working for a man you've all heard about—Al Capone. Al Capone wasn't famous for anything heroic, but he was notorious for the murders he'd committed and the illegal things he'd done.

Easy Eddie was Al Capone's lawyer, and he was very good. In fact, because of his skill, he was able to keep Al Capone out of jail.

To show his appreciation, Al Capone paid him very well. He not only earned big money, but he also would get extra things like a residence that filled an entire Chicago city block. The house was fenced, and he had live-in help and all the conveniences of the day.

Easy Eddie had a son. He loved his son and gave him all the best things while he was growing up—clothes, cars, and a good education. Because he loved his son, he tried to teach him right, but one thing he couldn't give his son was a good name and a good example.

Easy Eddie decided this was much more important than all the riches he had given his son. So he went to the authorities to rectify the wrong. To tell the truth, it meant he must testify against Al Capone, and he knew that Al Capone would do his best to have him killed.

Easy Eddie wanted most of all to try to be an example and to do the best he could to give a good name back to his son, so he testified. Within the year, he was shot down on a street in Chicago.

These sound like two unrelated stories, but Butch O'Hare was Easy Eddie's son.

—Unknown Author Found on multiple websites including www.inspirationalstories.com

AUTHOR'S INSIGHTS

Seeds that were planted: honesty, integrity, devotion, humility, love, and courage

Associated harvest: honor, inward strength, accomplishment, and affection

The yield was an understanding that courage is required as you press forward through life. It is often not easy but accomplishments of any measure will first require courage.

As you know, choosing the right direction is not easy; in fact, we reach one of the defining levels of maturity when we realize how our decisions affect those around us. This knowledge usually causes us to choose more carefully and sometimes differently.

YIELD IN ACTION NUMBER 19
DUTY

Sometimes we are called up to do our duty. There are incredible stories of those who selflessly serve in military duty. There are countless stories throughout history that can inspire us to know the value of doing our duty as members of the human family. One such story is told of a young man who lived in a small fishing village.

The Ship Wreck

One night, a storm caused a shipwreck off the coast of a small fishing town. When the alarm was sounded, the town's people went to the shore with their lanterns in typical fashion when such an event occurred. The light from the many lanterns was critical so that they could provide direction for the rescue boat to be able to find their way back to shore.

A team of men were quickly assembled, and they set out to rescue the stranded sailors. After battling the waves and struggling through the rain and wind, they finally made it back to the shore. The men explained that, "All but one man could fit into the rescue boat." The men that had gone on the first mission were too tired from fighting the waves to return for the one remaining crew member.

The leader of the village asked for volunteers for a second trip.

A young man stepped forward and offered his service. His mother pleaded, "Please don't go. Your father was killed at sea, and your brother has been missing at sea for weeks. You are the only child I have left. Please let the others go."

The young man felt it was his duty and something he had to do. He was the strongest young man remaining on the shore, so he, along with three others, made their way to the boat.

The rescue boat went back into the increasing darkness of the storm and soon faded out of sight.

Everyone waited and waited. The young man's mother feared the worst. Would she ever see her son again?

For what seemed an eternity, the rescue boat finally came back into view. In order to determine if more men were needed for another rescue attempt, a man shouted from the shore, "Did you get the other man?"

The young man shouted back, "Yes! And tell my mother it's my brother Bill."

—Unknown Author Found on multiple websites
including www.inspireme.net

AUTHOR'S INSIGHTS

Seeds that were planted: commitment, diligence, respect, duty, faith, and leadership

Associated harvest: honor, valor, and integrity

The yield was as we understand our duty, to God and mankind, we become more aware of others. As we serve others, significance will be added to the hallmarks by which we are known.

Duty is defined as "the force of moral obligation." Individuals with any military experience have learned to take their duty very seriously because another's life is depending on the accuracy at which they carry out their duty.

What duty do you have as a spouse, parent, or in your chosen profession? What duty do you simply have as a member of the human family?

We must be willing to step forward, travel away from the shore, and fight the storm to rescue another. A life may depend on you as someone who is prepared and has the strength to lead them to safety.

In this story, lanterns illuminated the shoreline and provided direction through the darkness for the rescuer's to find their way back to safety. You may be the brightest lantern in the life of those around you. You can be a beacon that provides direction and encouragement. A lighthouse that warns of dangerous activities that can destroy. A flood light that illuminates the pathways that leads to happiness and success.

Listen to your heart. When you do, you'll find ways to fulfill your duty to the fullest. It won't be easy. It may even be dark and scary at times. But your years of life have prepared you to help. When you generously give of yourself, you will realize the greatest personal rewards.

There is wisdom in the words of Marianne Williamson when she wrote,

> The purpose of our lives is to give birth to the best which is within us.

YIELD IN ACTION NUMBER 20

EMPATHY

Empathy allows you to understand another's situation and take action. Action is required in living a life of yield and empathy inspires you to act in the most meaningful way.

Wet Pants

Come with me to a third-grade classroom… There is a nine-year-old young boy sitting at his desk, and all of the sudden, there is a puddle between his feet and the front of his pants are wet.

He thinks his heart is going to stop because he cannot possibly imagine how this has happened. It's never happened before, and he knows when the boys find out, he will never hear the end of it. When the girls find out, they'll never speak to him again as long as he lives.

The boy believes his heart is going to stop. He put his head down on his desk and prays this prayer, "Dear God, this is an emergency! I need help now! Five minutes from now will be too late."

He looked up from his prayer, and here comes the teacher with a look in her eyes that says he has been discovered.

As the teacher is walking toward him, a classmate named Susie was carrying a goldfish bowl that was filled with water. Susie tripped in front of the teacher and inexplicably dumped the bowl of water in the boy's lap.

The boy pretended to be angry, but all the while, he is saying to himself, "Thank you, God! Thank you!"

Now all of the sudden, instead of being the object of ridicule, the boy is the object of sympathy. The teacher rushes him downstairs and gives him gym shorts to put on while his pants dry out. All the other children are on their hands and knees cleaning up around his desk.

The sympathy is wonderful. But as life would have it, the ridicule that should have been his, has been transferred to someone else—Susie.

She tries to help, but they tell her to get back. One student said, "You've done enough, you klutz!"

Finally, at the end of the day, as they were waiting for the bus, the boy walked over to Susie and whispers, "You did that on purpose, didn't you?"

Susie whispered back, "I wet my pants once too."

—Unknown Author Found on multiple websites including www.astrogems.com

AUTHOR'S INSIGHTS

Seeds that were planted: empathy, kindness, and devotion

Associated harvest: respect, admiration, love, and friendship

The yield was understanding that empathy calls for action to be taken. Sympathy will cause you to feel bad for another person's plight, but empathy will lead you to help where possible.

There are defining moments in our lifetime that shape and mold us. Our confidence can be compromised by one event, and our confidence can be enhanced by one event.

It is a vital role that you play in helping create a positive self-building experience for your family and all others who cross your path. You never know how one act of kindness will not only change an individual but will linger in their life forever and continue to affect the outcome of their success.

Therefore, intervene in an incident to protect another from a potentially embarrassing moment— even if it may transfer the focus to you. Your strength of character can handle it!

YIELD IN ACTION NUMBER 21

FRIENDSHIP

The following story, written by John W. Schlatter, is an example of how to recognize the needs of others and how to be a friend. As individuals we want to know we are accepted and needed. The following story shows just how important our friendship can be to others.

Kyle's Story

One day, when I was a freshman in high school, I saw a kid from my class walking home from school. His name was Kyle. It looked like he was carrying all his books. I thought to myself, *Why would anyone bring home all his books on a Friday? He must really be a nerd.* I had quite a weekend planned—a party and a football game with my friends—so I shrugged my shoulders and went on.

As I was walking, I saw a bunch of kids running toward him. They ran at him, knocking all his books out of his arms and tripped him, so he landed in the dirt. His glasses went flying, and I saw them land in the grass about ten feet from him. He looked up, and I saw this terrible sadness in his eyes. My heart went out to him. As I jogged over to him, I watched him crawl around looking for his glasses, and I saw a tear in his eye.

As I handed him his glasses, I said, "Those guys are jerks." He looked at me and said, "Hey, thanks!" There was a big smile on his face. It was one of those smiles that showed real gratitude. I helped him pick up his books and asked him where he lived. As it turned out, he lived near me, so I asked him why I had never seen him before. He said it was because he had previously attended a private school.

I would have never hung out with a private school kid before. We talked all the way home, and I helped carry his books. He seemed to be a pretty good kid. I asked him if he wanted to play football on Saturday with me and my friends. He said yes. The more I got to know Kyle, the more I liked him, and my friends thought the same of him.

Monday morning came, and there was Kyle with the huge stack of books again. I stopped him and said, "Man, you are really going to build some serious muscles with this pile of books!" He just laughed and handed me half the books.

Over the next four years, Kyle and I became best friends. When we were seniors, we began to think about college. Kyle decided on Georgetown, and I was going to Duke. I knew that we would always be friends, that the miles would never be a problem. He was going to be a doctor, and I was going for a degree in business on a football scholarship.

Kyle was valedictorian of our class. I teased him all the time about being a nerd. He had to prepare a speech for graduation. I was so glad it wasn't me having to get up there and speak.

Graduation day, I saw Kyle. He looked great. He was one of those guys that really found himself during high school. He filled out and actually looked good in glasses. He had more dates than me, and all the girls loved him! Boy, sometimes I was jealous.

Today was one of those days. I could see that he was nervous about his speech. So, I smacked him on the back and said, "Hey, big guy, you'll be great!" He looked at me and smiled with one of those looks. "Thanks," he said.

Later as he started his speech, he cleared his throat and began.

"Graduation is a time to thank those who helped you make it through those tough years. Your parents, your teachers, your siblings, maybe a coach... but mostly, your friends. I am here to tell all of you that being a friend to someone is the best gift you can give them. I am going to tell you a story."

I just looked at my friend with disbelief as he told the story of the first day we met. He had planned to kill himself over the weekend. He talked of how he had cleaned out his locker so his mom wouldn't have to do it later and was carrying his stuff home. He looked hard at me and gave me a little smile. "Thankfully, I was saved. My friend saved me from doing the unspeakable."

I heard the gasp go through the crowd as this handsome, popular boy told us all about his weakest moment. I saw his mom and dad looking at me and smiling that same grateful smile. Not until that moment, did I realize its depth.

AUTHOR'S INSIGHTS

Seeds that were planted: goodness, kindness, and respect

Associated harvest: gratitude, a miracle, and appreciation

The yield was learning that kindness at all times can turn the tide in every situation.

Never underestimate the power of your actions! It is just as important to realize that it may be something we didn't do that could have made all the difference. Consider the outcome of Kyle's story if Kyle had not made a new friend that day.

It may be a simple *hello*, an encouraging word or a congratulatory *good job* that can show your concern and influence. Your kindness and encouragement may seem very little at the time, but something powerful can result. You can save a life and not even know it.

YIELD IN ACTION NUMBER 22

PERSISTENCE

The key for any successful harvest is discipline. A farmer must be disciplined in cultivating the soil, planting at the right time of the season, and then following through with relentless nurturing of his crop. Brian Tracy tells us the same thing as it pertains to our personal development when he said, "Self-discipline is the key to personal greatness. It is the magic quality that opens all doors for you, and makes everything else possible. With self-discipline, the average person can rise as far and as fast as his talents and intelligence can take him. But without self-discipline, a person with every blessing of background, education, and opportunity will seldom rise above mediocrity."

The following story demonstrates a true test of an individual's willingness to be disciplined—even when there was no noticeable harvest in site.

Finding the New CEO

A successful businessman was growing older and knew it was time to choose a successor to take over the operations of his business. Instead of choosing one of his directors or his children, he decided to do something different. With no seemingly particular reason, he called all the young executives in his company together.

He said, "It is time for me to step down and choose the next CEO. I have decided to choose one of you to take over my position."

The young executives were shocked at the announcement as he continued, "I am going to give each one of you a seed today—one very special seed. I want you to plant the seed, water it, and come back here one year from today with what you have grown from the seed I have given you. I will then judge the plants that you bring, and the one I choose will be the next CEO."

One man named Jim, like the others, received a seed. He went home and excitedly, told his wife the story. She helped him get a pot, soil and compost, and he planted the seed. Every day, he would water it and watch to see if it had grown. After about three weeks, some of the other executives began to talk about their seeds and the plants that were beginning to grow.

Jim kept checking his seed, but nothing ever grew.

Three weeks, four weeks, five weeks went by, still nothing.

By now, others were talking about their plants, but Jim didn't have a plant, and he felt like a failure.

Six months went by—still nothing in Jim's pot. He feared that somehow he had killed his seed. Everyone else had trees and tall plants, but he had nothing. Jim didn't ever have anything to say to his colleagues about the progress of his seed. He just kept watering and fertilizing the soil, hoping that something would begin to grow.

A year finally went by, and all the young executives of the company were to bring their plants to the CEO for inspection.

Jim told his wife that he wasn't going to take an empty pot, but she asked him to be honest about what happened. Jim felt sick to his stomach. It was going to be the most embarrassing moment of his life, but he knew his wife was right. He took his empty pot to the board room. When Jim arrived, he was amazed at the variety of plants grown by the other executives. They were beautiful, arriving in all shapes and sizes. Jim put his empty pot on the floor. Some of his colleagues felt sorry for him, while others laughed.

When the CEO arrived, he surveyed the room and greeted his young executives.

Jim just tried to hide in the back. "My, what great plants, trees, and flowers you have grown," said the CEO. "Today, one of you will be appointed the next CEO."

All of a sudden, the CEO spotted Jim at the back of the room with his empty pot. He asked the financial director to bring him to the front. Jim was terrified. He thought, *The CEO knows I've failed at this assignment. He probably thinks I didn't follow his instructions or try at all. Maybe he will have me fired?*

When Jim got to the front, the CEO asked him what had happened to his seed. Jim told him the story.

The CEO asked everyone to sit down except Jim. He looked at Jim, and then turned and announced to the young executives, "Behold, your next chief executive officer! His name is Jim!"

Jim couldn't believe it.

"How could he be the new CEO?" the others said. "He couldn't grow anything from his seed."

Then the CEO said, "One year ago today, I gave everyone in this room a seed. I told you to take the seed, plant it, water it, and bring it back to me today. But I gave you all boiled seeds. They were dead. It was not possible for them to grow.

"All of you, except Jim, have brought me trees and plants and flowers. When you found that the seed would not grow, you substituted another seed for the one I gave you. Jim was the only one with the courage and honesty to bring me a pot with my seed in it. Therefore, he is the one who will be the new chief executive officer!"

—Unknown Author Found on multiple
websites including www.inspirationalstories.com

AUTHOR'S INSIGHTS

Seeds that were planted: honesty, courage, commitment, leadership, and humility

Associated harvest: promotion, integrity, and appreciation

The yield was an understanding that when we remain true to our character, we can confidently live each day with no concern of who we are supposed to be.

You must be able to discover the most important seed-to-harvest relationships that can help you achieve the highest yield in your life and organization.

Remember,

> If you plant honesty, you will reap trust.
> If you plant goodness, you will reap friendships.
> If you plant humility, you will reap greatness.
> If you plant perseverance, you will reap contentment.
> If you plant consideration, you will reap perspective.
> If you plant hard work, you will reap success.
> If you plant forgiveness, you will reap reconciliation.

The key is that you must have the self-discipline to plant and nurture positive character traits. When you do, the rest is guaranteed to take care of itself.

YIELD IN ACTION NUMBER 23

KINDNESS

The seed of kindness may have the greatest return and may influence your harvest and yield more than anything else. Just be nice. Just do the right thing.

It Pays to Return Kindness

His name was Fleming, and he was a poor Scottish farmer. One day, while trying to make a living for his family, he heard a cry for help coming from a nearby bog. He dropped his tools and ran to the bog.

There, mired to his waist in black muck, was a terrified boy, screaming and struggling to free himself.

Farmer Fleming saved the lad from what could have been a slow and terrifying death.

The next day, a fancy carriage pulled up to the Scotsman's sparse surroundings, and an elegantly dressed nobleman stepped out and introduced himself as the father of the boy farmer Fleming saved.

"I want to repay you," said the nobleman. "You saved my son's life."

"No, I can't accept payment for what I did," the Scottish farmer replied. At that moment, the farmer's own son came to the door of the family hovel.

"Is that your son?" the nobleman asked.

"Yes," the farmer replied proudly.

"I'll make you a deal. Let me provide him with the level of education my own son will enjoy. If the lad is anything like his father, he'll no doubt grow to be a man we both will be proud of." And that he did.

Farmer Fleming's son attended the very best schools and, in time, graduated from St. Mary's Hospital Medical School in London and went on to become known throughout the world as the noted Sir Alexander Fleming, the discoverer of penicillin.

Years afterward, the same nobleman's son who was saved from the bog was stricken with pneumonia.

What saved his life this time? Penicillin.

The name of the nobleman? Lord Randolph Churchill. His son's name?

Sir Winston Churchill.

—Unknown Author Found on multiple websites including www.storiesonline.com

AUTHOR'S INSIGHTS

Seeds that were planted: hard work, dedication, loyalty, and kindness

Associated harvest: prosperity, respect, and gratitude

The yield was realizing that when we do what is right with no expected reward, we will find our deepest self-respect and joy.

You never know what good will come of our kindness. Look for ways to serve others with no expected reward. Just do the right thing.

Kindness is a character trait that should be one of the hallmarks by which we are known.

YIELD IN ACTION NUMBER 24

PASSION

I don't have to look any further than by my side to find one of the greatest examples of yield. This is a very personal story because it is about my wife, Toni. She has taught dance for thirty years and owned her dance school for twenty-three of those years. It was a long standing tradition that her Spring Recital was held on Mother's Day weekend. As this particular dance year came to a close, two stories are worthy of telling.

Remembering a Friend

The first is about my wife. This story began about fifteen years ago when one of her good friends died from repertory complications caused by the hantavirus. Her friend's daughter was a dance student and only eight years old at the time. That year, my wife started a scholarship program in her honor—The Cheri Newbold Scholarship Fund.

Cheri was a great supporter of the dance program and friend to my wife. The idea of the scholarship was to honor Cheri's compassionate character but also allow donations to be made that could be distributed to students who might not otherwise be able to participate.

A desiring student writes a letter to apply for the scholarship, and within the letter, they need to explain why they should be one of the recipients. This process is completed at the end of the current dance year so that the scholarship can be applied to next year's tuition and costumes. Based on the need, varying dollar amounts are awarded.

Donations helped fund the scholarship for the first few years, but for at least the last ten years, my wife has been the sole contributor. She has wanted to maintain the memory of her friend. No one but me has known of her goodness in keeping the scholarship alive. She is a remarkable example of friendship, and I love and admire her for her kindness and devotion to students who want to dance.

With that background, the second part of the story pertains to this year's scholarship recipients.

At the end of the recital, all the students filed on to the stage to take their final bows. After everyone was on stage and the applause subsided, my wife took the microphone. She recognized her teachers for their work, acknowledged the departing seniors, handed out the teacher's Star Awards, and then announced the scholarship winners.

The first recipient was a current student who worked to pay her own dance tuition. She is a great young lady and one who was deserving of help. Then, my wife told the audience that she wanted to read a letter from a scholarship applicant. She read,

Dear Dance in the Rockies Staff,

I know I am seven days late [in turning my letter in after the deadline for the scholarship], and I wish I were not. See, as I write I want to spin. I want to dance. I want to move. I live in a world of dancers [friends, who attend your school]. I spend my days watching girls leap, spin do their jazz dances, talk about dance. My whole life I wanted to dance, but I haven't. My older sister, Cypress, has Down syndrome and my younger sister, Sophie, had a heart transplant and passed. With all the medical bills, food, housing, and clothing costs, my parents never could afford dance.

Can I dance too? I will be the most responsible young lady. I have all the dance clothing, thanks to hand-me-downs. I will be on time, I will be at all the classes, and I will behave and pay attention. Dancing is my outlet for my feelings.

> I just love it when I leap in the air and land on my feet. When I spin and feel dizziness. I really, really want to be in Dance. People say I have legs of a dancer. Dance is a passion to me. It would be extravagant if on Sunday, you called my name for the scholarship. Please, I want to dance. I am the right one for the scholarship.
>
> Love, a want-to-be dancer,
> Vivien

Through my wife's tears, Vivien's name was called as a recipient of an eight-hundred-dollar scholarship. This will pay for two classes, all associated costs and costumes. Vivien was in the audience, and my wife invited her to join her friends and the other dancers on the stage. The students, teachers, and audience shared her tears and a standing ovation was given to this twelve-year-old girl who captured all our hearts.

Passion will make Vivien a great dancer. Passion is one of the most important character traits found in those who live a life of yield. Passion will make seeds grow faster and your harvest more bountiful.

Very importantly, Tim Connor made this compelling statement when he said, "Passion is the great equalizer. It can make up for a lack of experience and knowledge."

May you be passionate about the things that matter most to you. May you find ways to make a difference in your own home and in the farthest reaches of your personal and professional activities.

YIELD IN ACTION NUMBER 25

LEGACY

As I was completing this book, I sent it to my friend Tony Kovach who is the editor and owner of a sales and industry training magazine for builders. I provide a monthly article for his publication. In the midst of him providing edits for this book, I submitted the article below for an upcoming monthly article. He suggested that it be included in the book. I agreed as it is my story of two of the greatest people to have blessed my life—my dad and mom.

The Greatest Man and Woman I've Ever Known

My father is the greatest man I've ever known. I want to tell you a few things about him that continue to influence the way I live my life and conduct my business activities. He truly lived a life of yield, and I'm proud to be his son.

My father was the kind of man who would never compromise or stray from giving his customer's the best products, the best value, and the best service possible. He owned the grocery store in our little town of six hundred residents, but this small community store reached farming and ranching clientele throughout the entire region.

As you can imagine, I always had a job, especially in the summer when school was out. My siblings and

I helped mop and wax the floors on weekends, and we were taught how to work in every department so that if someone was sick or on vacation, we were able to fill in where needed. These were the days of paper bags and the days when every customer's groceries were delivered to their car. These were the days when full-service gas stations were on every corner; self-service pumping was not even a consideration. Ah, the good old days of customer service at its best!

Some of my most memorable customer service moments occurred when no customer was even nearby. The first occurred on a hot summer day. I was working at the front end of the store bagging groceries and carrying them out to customer's cars.

I was probably in junior high school, and the cashier's began to notice that the ice cream was soft. They called my father from the back of the store, and he quickly found that the freezer was not working. Normally when this happened, we would move the ice cream into shopping carts and roll them into the walk-in freezer. Once the ice cream freezer was fixed, we could move the ice cream back into the store.

On this particular day, my father felt that the ice cream had thawed too much and while it could be refrozen and sold, it was not suitable for his customers. I can remember unloading the freezer and then throwing the entire freezer full of ice cream away in the Dumpster behind the store. I'm sure the loss was greater than the profits he would have made for a couple of days, but his commitment to excellence was uncompromising.

I think today that on that occasion he may have been teaching his son a valuable lesson, even if it meant a loss of profit. The store was a place to make a living, but it was more importantly a place to raise his children.

I can also remember my father would sell a custom cut quarter or a half of beef through the store, and it always had a tenderness guarantee. I can remember two occasions when someone brought their beef back and asked for a replacement. No questions were asked. The beef was replaced, and he made sure the weight was more than the previous purchase.

I can remember the huge scale that was used to make sure the amount of meat returned was weighed so that there was no question that they were being treated fairly when they came back to pick up the replacement.

I can further remember the next night, and many more nights thereafter, when our family would eat the returned beef for dinner so that my father could test the quality of what he had sold. I can't remember if it was tough or not, but I do remember that he never questioned the customer's opinion—his customers would have the best product he could possibly provide to them.

There seemed to be an unwritten, controlling question to every answer about quality, price, and service: are we earning our customer's loyalty and trust with every interaction and every purchase?

I was two years old when my father and mother bought the grocery store. My father lost his battle with cancer over twenty years ago, and he is talked about with great admiration still today. To give you one quick example of his contribution to the community, I was told by a city official once that the store collected approximately 80 percent of all the city's sales tax revenue. He helped fund nearly all the cities growth and economic stability.

After his passing, the library in town was just being built, and the city council voted unanimously to have it named after him. I had occasion to visit the library a couple of weeks ago, and tears filled my eyes again as I saw his picture on the wall and reread the tribute to his life.

He did not learn his customer service insight through an MBA program. In fact, he didn't learn it in college or high school. I know this because my father did not finish beyond the tenth grade. He was a high-school drop out, but yet he was wise, and he understood the need to plant and continually nurture the seeds of success on a daily basis.

It doesn't take an education to be successful; it takes an educated heart. For this and many more things, I'm grateful to my father for showing me the greatest lessons of life.

———◆———

My mom is the greatest woman I've ever known. She was the unsung hero who worked behind the scenes at the store. She kept the books, but more importantly she stood beside my father in all his business ideas. She worked wherever needed throughout the store and helped make it successful.

One place that her service is impossible to enumerate is the work she performed within the walls of her home and the sacrifices she made on behalf of her children. I was involved in sports as I went through school, and even though my mom was busy at the store, my uniforms were always clean and ready for me on game day. I'm sure this demanded some late nights, but she did whatever it took to care for her family. I remember my mom would prepare a special meal for me before home games, and she would then be in the stands saving a place for my dad. Just before the first play of the game, my dad would walk in and sit next to her. She kept our home and lives in order.

Today, at eighty-eight years old, she is still serving the community by delivering meals on wheels with my sister Cindy. She donates her time to the library each week and because she is one of the oldest lifelong residents of our community, she is the one called upon as a member of the Historical Society to answer questions about our community or its previous residents. She willingly and readily serves wherever possible.

A great tribute to my mom took place this year. While she is still alive, the library board wanted to also recognize her lifelong commitment to the community just as they did years ago for my father. She took her rightful place next to my father as they renamed the community room after both of them. It is now the McClanahan Community Room.

I once heard that just as we have the Statue of Liberty on the East Coast to remind us of our freedom, we need another bookend or a Statue of Integrity that would rightfully be planted in a harbor on the West Coast. These two statues would mark the two great characteristics that this nation was founded upon.

If such a statue was commissioned, and an artist was selected for such a task, my mom and dad would be perfect figures to represent this character trait and to be chiseled out of stone.

Great service and noticeable integrity is within all of our reach and are the hallmarks by which our life and businesses should be known. Further, we would be reminded that the power of working together has produced our greatest results as a nation.

My parents planted the seeds of hard work, service, support, compassion, commitment, love, tenderness, and a host of other seeds in their lives and in my life. They may not have known it at the time, but their harvest is a lasting legacy of greatness and their yield is bounteous.

I love you both so much!

SUMMATION

When you learn how to apply the experiences and examples of others into your own life, you can more rapidly improve your yield. The examples in this chapter are just a scratch on the surface of greatness that is all around you.

One of the great seeds you must plant in your life is the seed of observation. Be open to the many learning opportunities all around you on a daily basis. Combining these opportunities with your own experiences will set you on the way toward building and living a life with yield in mind.

Your current safe boundaries were once unknown frontiers.

—Anonymous

One machine can do the work of fifty ordinary men. No machine can do the work of one extraordinary man.

—Elbert Hubbard

The highest reward for a person's toil is not what they get for it, but what they become by it.

—John Ruskin

MOVING FORWARD

In the companies I have owned, I wanted to find a way to create an environment that supported enduring success and created a culture of optimism. I wanted to provide a means by which ongoing nurturing of the positive seeds I'd planted could reveal the greatest yield. I wanted to continually realize a greater yield organizationally, but I equally wanted to see my employees reach their highest personal potential.

There are organizations that exist today and were formed out of a desire to provide a simplified means of communicating and encouraging an understanding of the principles that influence our lives. Their mission is to inspire greatness and encourage the mastery of the skills that promote personal excellence. Their mission is to help individuals and organizations sustain a pattern of ongoing growth.

Through the Internet and other creative mediums, there are improved means of distribution of and accessibility to, the principles, patterns, and pathways to the character traits associated with successful individuals. These platforms make it possible for even the busiest individual to have time to be inspired by positive, reinforcing personal development ideas.

As demonstrated in the previous chapter, we can enhance our understanding of how to achieve a more bountiful harvest and greater yield by seeing how others live their lives. When you can connect instructional information to a practical example, you are more easily able to make the skill more applicable in your own life. These short inspirational stories reinforce core values, encourage positive attitudes, and promote personal growth. Information is great, but application is king.

It is important to create an environment that supports a disciplined and consistent exposure to these success principles. According to Steve Siebold, author of *Secrets of the World Class*, "Discipline is the watchword of great performers. Discipline makes the difference between the good and the great."

A seminar, for example, may be a good jumpstart for you when learning new skills, however, consistent exposure to success principles and patterns is required over an extended period of time in order to support the mastery of any skill. Again, there are many great organizations that provide the extended exposure, at a consistent frequency so that mastery can take place. I encourage you to frequently visit www.lawoftheyield. com for ongoing support of your quest for a greater yield in your life.

Aristotle said, "We are what we repeatedly do. Excellence, then is not an act, but a habit."

If you hired a personal trainer to help you get in shape, you could more easily meet your physical goals because you would be forced to maintain consistency and discipline. The trainer spends hours behind the scenes creating, monitoring, and adjusting your work out program and planning your meals. Your success still depends on you. You must follow the plan, but the work has been reduced for you so that implementation is more manageable and achievable. In like manner, you must align yourself and your organization with an appropriate professional and organizational leadership development curriculum/program.

Just like a gentle rain provides the best irrigation for a crop to flourish, a carefully planned personal or organizational development curriculum will introduce one success principle that is followed by another and continues to reinforce all previously learned ideas. There are constants in human interaction and you must continue to reinforce their significance and application until they are mastered and become an inherent part of your character.

I'm sure you've heard the three keys to purchasing real estate: location, location, location. Well, you'll now hear the three keys to managing your attitude and realizing your greatest potential for growth: reinforce, reinforce, reinforce.

You are privileged to be able to set the direction of your own sail and determine whether you will go east or if you will go west. Your course is not determined by the wind but rather by the set of your sail. To stay your course through calm days and days filled with challenges, it is not up to the wind—it is up to you!

My greatest desire is that you will enjoy a
Bounteous Harvest.